God bless you.

Fr. Maurice McNeely

Catholicism without the

GUILT

By Father Maurice McNeely

Catholicism without the Guilt
All Rights Reserved
Copyright © 2006 Father Maurice G. McNeely

Outskirts Press
http://www.outskirtspress.com

ISBN-10: 1-59800-764-5
ISBN-13: 978-1-59800-764-0

Library of Congress Control Number: 2006936567

Outskirts Press and the "OP" logo are trademarks belonging to
Outskirts Press, Inc.

Printed in the United States of America

WARNING:
If the jacket of this book or slang
words offend you,
do not read any further!

A professor I once knew had this to say about the teaching of others: "Challenge them; make them think; cause them to laugh. That's the atmosphere that leads to wisdom." If that's true, Father McNeely has indeed provided the atmosphere. The wisdom part is up to us.

Fr. Paul L. Bianchi

Catholicism without the Guilt is a practical approach to our Catholic faith. I highly recommend it, especially for young adults.

Chaplain, Colonel Owen Mullen
U.S. Army, retired

Special Acknowledgments

Without the encouragement and constant input from Daniel S.H. Mew and my sister, Margaret "Peggy" A. Mara, this book would never have been written. It is because of their encouragement that this book came about. I will be forever grateful.

Three other people whom I am humbly indebted to are the late Fr. Raymond "Holtzie" Holtz, the late Ralph Schmelzer, and Fr. John "Jack" Owens. Without their spiritual support and tutorial skills, I would never have been ordained; but, then, Holtzie would say, "Don't blame me!"

Sincerely yours in Christ,
Fr. Maurice G. McNeely

Table of Contents

		Page
Foreword		
Introduction		
Chapter 1:	Your Conscience Is Supreme	1
Chapter 2:	No One Has a Monopoly on God	11
Chapter 3:	Don't Worship Any Book, Not Even the Bible	25
Chapter 4:	The Eight Sacraments (Part 1)	37
Chapter 5:	The Eight Sacraments (Part 2)	51
Chapter 6:	Sex and Sexuality (The Good Stuff)	63
Chapter 7:	Social Issues and Tragedies of Our Time	81
Chapter 8:	I Believe! (… or Do I?)	99
Chapter 9:	Gambling, Alcohol, Drugs, and Swearing	107
Chapter 10:	Exploring Different Religious Ideas	115
Chapter 11:	Everything Else You Wanted to Know about Catholicism but Never Had the Chance to Ask (Part 1)	115

Chapter 12:   Everything Else You Wanted to
               Know about Catholicism but Never
               Had the Chance to Ask (Part 2)   145

Chapter 13:   Magic Numbers, "the Rapture,"
               Psychics, and Ouija Boards   157

Conclusion   165

Foreword

Many Catholics have either attended Catechism, religious education instruction, or a parochial school. Most of the certified or lay teachers, nuns, or priests were good and sincere people, but they didn't have the knack for explaining the Catholic faith in a language that we all could understand. Many times, if we asked a difficult question, they thought that we were just trying to be "smart asses" or that we were trying to stump them. But we were honestly looking for logical answers. And so, after being in the priesthood for over 48 years and in response to the many requests from my parishioners, I decided to write *Catholicism* without the Guilt.

I love the Catholic faith with all my heart and soul, and I would never intend any disrespect toward it. What I have tried to do through this book is to answer some of these questions in a common, logical order. I hope *Catholicism without the Guilt* will reinforce the idea of God's unconditional love for each of us and to let us know that we can always question the Catholic faith without any form of retribution, that our personal conscience is supreme, and that we should feel free to follow it. And if you make the effort, you will discover the truth because Jesus wants us to be free from worry. Our Catholic faith puts us in personal contact with Jesus, both physically and spiritually, through Holy Communion. It is the true link to Jesus and it helps us to understand the meaning of life and what it means to love God and our neighbors as we love ourselves.

I wrote *Catholicism without the Guilt* to honor the more than one billion Roman Catholics in the world, to help the 67 million Catholics in the United States, and to bring home the 17 million lapsed Catholics so that they might understand their faith a little better. And if this book could allow those of other religious faiths or those who are nonreligious to open their hearts to God too, then I think we all will live with a better understanding about what this moment on earth — our life — is all about. God loves us more than we love ourselves; this is true not just for Catholics but for everyone equally. Now, isn't that "the good news"?

Aloha pauole (love never fails),
Fr. Maurice G. McNeely

Figure 2. Graphic layout by Daniel S.H. Mew.

Introduction

The cover for this book is similar to a poster that I put up in Vietnam to get the young GIs to attend Mass. The one difference was that, instead of Adam and Eve wearing fig leaves, I used a photo of a Playboy centerfold, something like what the GIs had pinned on their walls. My poster worked well. Everyone knew that Mass was at 5:30 p.m., and each week I did something a little different. One of my posters said, "Get Your Ass to Mass." Another week, I put little labels on the urinals in the restrooms and on the floors nearby the toilets. The labels said "SEX" in bold letters and then, below, in tiny print: "Mass at 5:30 p.m." I remember the Major calling me into his office to tell me he thought the labels were disgusting and in poor taste. But then I asked him, "What time is Mass?"

He said, "5:30 p.m."

And I said, "Case closed, Sir," (after which I proceeded to inquire as to what exactly he had been doing on the floor of the men's room that he could read the tiny print).

Now that I've got your attention, I need to tell you that I am neither a scholar nor a theologian. I am just a simple parish priest, now retired. In this book, I will be quoting scholars and eminent theologians, but the rest are my own personal views. Actually, I was lucky that I got ordained at all because my grade point average was less than stellar, to say the least. The reason for this goes back to the Catholic hang-ups most of us grew up with. Ever since I was a little boy attending Catholic school, I was taught about the lives of the saints (some very strange people, to be sure). They were held up as the people we were supposed to emulate. One was the Cure of Ars, the Patron Saint of Parish Priests. He was wonderful at hearing confessions, but he was an awful student: He flunked all his tests and was terrible at Latin. In spite of that — or perhaps because of it — he was revered as a model priest. So I thought to myself, *This must be what I have to do to be a priest worthy of sainthood.* And from then on, I did everything in my power to fail my classes, and I did an outstanding job of it, so much so, that I almost didn't get ordained.

Thinking back, I regret taking literally so much of what the priests and nuns said. For instance, I was always told, "God sends crosses to people whom He loves." So, whenever things in my life were going well (a sure sign that God loved me very much), I would get a little panicky because, as I had been taught, I was sure God was just waiting for the perfect moment to screw me over. But nothing could be further from the truth. God doesn't want to screw anyone over. He loves everyone too much to do anything like that. In fact, the main purpose of me writing this book is to let you know that God loves you more than you love yourself, that He created you in this time and place to share His love, and that He loves you unconditionally. He would never abandon you. If you don't want Him in your life, then you, alone, will have to reject Him. Please always keep that in mind. If that lesson is the one thing that you take away from reading this book, then I will be forever grateful.

By the way, the title of my book — *Catholicism without the Guilt* — comes from the fact that many Catholics harbor an inordinate amount of guilt, feeling they somehow missed the mark in their relationship with God or the Church. I am not sure if all this came about by accident. I think that many of the clergy — bishops, priests, brothers, and nuns — and even our parents thought it was a good thing for us to have guilt. They were going to get us to heaven if they had to send us to hell to do it. That kind of argument just doesn't make sense, but we were too afraid to question such things.

Before the Second Vatican Council in 1962, the Church seemed to have a rule for just about everything in our religious lives, and all of that just added to our guilt when we sometimes slipped, occasionally because we didn't have the necessary will power and other times because of sheer forgetfulness. For example, if you were going to receive Holy Communion, you weren't allowed to eat or drink anything, not even water, from midnight on. Many children couldn't make their first Holy Communion with their classmates because they had forgotten this rule and had taken a sip of water. Also, women had to wear a hat — and those who forgot would use Kleenex or even a piece of toilet paper as a substitute — because they weren't supposed to enter a church with their heads exposed. Futhermore, it was considered a mortal sin if a wife refused to have sex with her husband, even if she was sick, worn-out, or already had 10 children.

When I was first ordained, the Church had a rule that only the priest could touch the host (or wafer) in Holy Communion, and even then, we could use only a thumb and forefinger. One day when I was distributing Holy Communion, I accidentally dropped the host down the opening of a woman's dress. I was mortified. Because she wasn't allowed to touch the host, she proceeded to jump up and down until it fell onto the floor. What a nightmare! All these rules from the Catholic Church were meant to instill respect, but they, instead, generated fear. And they distracted us from what was really important.

Today, people's guilt can arise from a different source. In our society, we now openly talk about a host of previously taboo subjects, including abortion, birth control, capital punishment, ordination of women to the priesthood, the right of gays and lesbians to marry and adopt children, and so on. All of these are legitimate issues for discussion, but many Catholics still feel guilty for even thinking about such topics. Well, they shouldn't, and the Church has a duty from Christ to help people sort through such issues so that they can decide for themselves how best to lead their lives. To that cause, *Catholicism without the Guilt* is my small contribution.

Chapter 1
Your Conscience Is Supreme

A man who died went before St. Peter and asked, "May I pass into heaven?"

St. Peter questioned the man, "How did you die?"

"Well," said the young man, "when I was alive, I worked nights and on one particular morning, I came home early to find my wife sitting in the living room wearing a fancy negligee, and there were two empty wine glasses on the coffee table. I was suspicious, so I asked her what was going on. She seemed nervous as she said, 'Nothing.' I looked all over the apartment for other clues. When I went out on the balcony, I saw a young man in the backyard below, putting his pants on. I got so angry that I grabbed the first thing I could get my hands on, which was the refrigerator, and pushed it over the balcony. It landed on the man and killed him. At my trial, they sentenced me to death, and that's why I'm here before you today."

St. Peter said, "I understand. You were merely acting in a fit of anger. You may enter the gates of heaven."

Soon after, another young man came before St. Peter, asking to pass through heaven's gate. St. Peter inquired of him, "How did you die?"

The young man replied, "You won't believe this, but while I was getting ready for work one morning, I had to get my pants from the backyard clothesline and suddenly, a refrigerator fell on me, squashing me to death!"

St. Peter said, "What a horrible accident. You surely may enter heaven."

Then a third young man came before St. Peter and asked to enter heaven. When he was asked how he had died, he explained, "Well, one day, I was just sitting inside this refrigerator and some son-of-a-bitch pushed it off a third-floor balcony!"

All joking aside, the purpose of this story is to illustrate how God knows everything that goes on. In other words, you can't fool Him. He understands you better than you will ever understand yourself. As you will hear me repeat over and over throughout this book, God is on your side so there is no need to be dishonest with Him or try to deceive Him.

That said, God also doesn't want your blind obedience. That statement might seem to contradict things that we were taught as kids. Ever since I was a young Catholic, I was told that I had to take things on faith, to accept anything that an authority figure in the church prescribed. Whenever I asked a question that was difficult to answer, the priest or nun would claim that I didn't have faith. But what that response actually meant was that they just didn't have an answer.

The most important thing that I can relate to you is this: God loves us more than we love ourselves. He judges us by our conscience, not by the Church's conscience or our parents' conscience, but by our own personal conscience. Simply put, the individual's conscience is supreme. This belief has been — and will probably always be — the best-kept secret of the Catholic faith. So please forgive me when I repeat it throughout this book, but it is so important that it warrants being said more than once.

Now I would like to quote from his holiness, Pope John Paul II, in his book, *Crossing the Threshold of Hope*. There he wrote, "If man is admonished by his conscience, even if an erroneous conscience, but one whose voice appears to him unquestionably true, he must always listen to it."[1] That statement doesn't sound like the Pope we knew because of his long history of insisting that Catholics always follow the official teaching of the Church. But if you really pinned him

---

[1] His Holiness John Paul II, *Crossing the Threshold of Hope*. New York: Alfred A. Knopf. 1999. p.191.

down on the subject, he would admit that the bottom line was freedom of conscience.

Ever since I can remember, I was taught that God can do anything, but I would venture to say that that's not quite true. There are three things that God can't do. First, He can't do anything wrong. Second, He can't contradict Himself, like painting Himself into a corner. When I was a kid, I would ask the nuns, "Is there anything God can't do?"

They always responded with, "God can do anything!"

I would smile and then ask, "If so, could God make a rock so heavy that even He couldn't lift it?" I would always get them with that one, smart-ass that I was.

Finally, God can't make us do anything we don't want to do. Once He made us human beings in His image and gave us free will, He gave up His ability to interfere.

As Americans, we have always held personal freedom to be our greatest treasure, something worth fighting for. In fact, many wars have resulted from some people thinking they can deny others the God-given gift of free will. But those people are ultimately only fooling themselves. Any victories to squash an individual's free will can only be temporary. Of course, free will is a beautiful gift, but it's also what gives people the ability to screw each other over. The events of September 11, 2001, happened because those individuals who were responsible had the gift of free will, no matter how inhumanely applied. But God didn't will that tragedy to occur. He can't manipulate the will of any individual or group of persons who wish to commit such horrific acts. If He were, indeed, able to control our wills, then we would cease to be human beings.

Similarly, God does not will the death and destruction associated with disasters of nature. Such events simply occur as part of the natural rhythms of our physical world. When lightning strikes a forest, for instance, the resulting fire might destroy many plants, animals, and even some humans, but the process could serve a greater good, enabling the ecosystem to rejuvenate itself when it eventually recovers. With all this in mind, ask yourself, would you personally wish God to take away your free will, to take away one of the primary ingredients that makes you human, to transform you into an irrational animal?

Here I've been talking about "God" without defining what I think that term means. I should be careful because different words mean different things to different people. One of my favorite Scripture quotes is found only in the King James Bible, which states in Acts 9:5, "And he said, Who art thou, Lord? And the Lord said, I am Jesus whom thou persecutest: It is hard for thee to kick against the pricks." Many times I'd say to people, "I thought of you when I read this Scripture," even though I doubt that this was what Jesus had in mind. Suffice it to say, before beginning any dialogue, it's important that you define your terms and that all participants are on the same page. You can't get anywhere in a discussion with someone if you and that person are using the same terms, but talking about two completely different things.

When I use the word "God," I mean the Supreme Intelligence, the Uncreated Creator, the All-Powerful, All-Knowing, and All-Loving that always was — and always will be — existing in the eternal now. Catholicism teaches that God is a being who is *divine in nature* ("nature" meaning the essential attributes that define what a thing is).

There are, of course, other categories of nature. There is *human nature*. Beings of this type are born in time and die in time: They walk, they talk, they have free will, and they are responsible for their actions. There is also *animal nature*. Beings of this type are born and die like humans, but they do not have free will. You wouldn't put a dog in jail for stealing something because it doesn't have the ability to reason between right and wrong. There is also *inanimate nature*. A rock, for example, isn't born and doesn't die. It just sits there (kind of like some of the kids I knew in school). Plants, too, have their own nature that includes being alive, but having no free will (as humans do) nor any intelligence (as animals do).

Now, returning to the subject of divine nature, or God, this concept is of the utmost importance to this book because if

4

divine nature, or God, doesn't exist, then the rest of what I have to say doesn't matter. But no one can prove to you that God exists other than you, yourself.

Albert Einstein came to his own conclusions over a lifetime of observations. He said that the universe isn't a crapshoot. It's too complicated. Nature is too well-ordered and organized. Just look at the human body and all of its marvels. Consider the two Bose speakers (namely, your ears) that you have on the sides of your head, the two high-definition color televisions (your eyes), and the device (your nose) that enables you to enjoy all the great smells of food and nature while also protecting you from harmful substances.

Scientists say that the hairs in your nose filter 35 pounds of oxygen every day, and without them, a person with sensitive allergies could choke to death. Think about your mouth and its ability to taste all the great foods you enjoy, as well as its ability to kiss. And what about your skin and the sensual feelings it transmits — your sexuality and all the pleasure you can give to and receive from others? How could this all happen by chance? Just one of these complex systems (your ears, for instance) might happen by chance, but even then, I doubt it. And the mathematical probability of each of these wondrous systems — all functioning together in beautiful harmony — occurring randomly in a single human birth seems impossible.

Now, I know that many people will argue that all living things are the product of evolution — the theory that the various types of animals and plants have their origins in other preexisting types, and that the distinguishable differences are due to modifications in successive generations. And I believe they are correct on some level. Indeed, the Catholic Church has long looked favorably on evolution. In 1950, Pope Pius XII called the theory a "serious hypothesis" worthy of study, and as early as the 5th century, St. Augustine warned against a literal reading of the Genesis creation account. Pope John Paul II went even further than his predecessors in declaring that a convergence of scientific evidence gathered in the past 50 years made a significant argument in favor of evolution. But even then, the theory of evolution can't explain how life itself began, nor, for that matter, has science been able to completely solve the mystery of how the universe came into existence.

Interestingly, the first person to postulate the Big Bang theory — the idea that the universe originated billions of years ago from a single dense point of nearly infinite energy — was a Catholic priest: Fr. Georges Lemaitre. He first proposed the theory in 1927, and two years later, at Mt. Wilson Observatory in California, the American astronomer, Edwin Hubble, discovered that galaxies were moving away from one other at tremendous speeds, confirming Lemaitre's theory.

Later, none other than Albert Einstein, a personal friend of Fr. Lemaitre, said that Lemaitre's theory was the most beautiful and satisfactory explanation of creation he had ever heard. Lemaitre's theory, the idea that a burst of fireworks marked the beginning of time and space in "a day without yesterday," was a radical departure from the prevailing scientific understandings, but it has since become the most probable explanation of the universe.

In 1998, when scientists at U.C. Berkeley discovered that the universe was expanding at an increasing rate, Stephen W. Hawking, a brilliant theoretical physicist and one of the world's greatest minds, said the finding was too preliminary to be taken seriously. Later, though, he changed his mind: "I have now had more time to consider the observations, and they look quite good. This led me to reconsider my theoretical prejudices." Hawking was actually being modest. In the face of the scientific turmoil caused by the supernovae results, he had adapted quickly. The phrase "theoretical prejudices" makes one think of the attitudes that hampered scientists 70 years ago. It took a mathematician who also happened to be a Catholic priest to look at the evidence with an open mind and create a model that worked.[2] In Hawking's bestselling book, *A Brief*

---

[2] Mark Midbon, "A Day without Yesterday: Georges Lemaitre & the Big Bang" in *Catholic Educator's Resource Center,*

History of Time, he states that,

Science seems to have uncovered a set of laws that, within the limits set by the uncertainty principle, tell us how the universe will develop with time, if we know its state at any one time. These laws may have originally been decreed by God, but it appears that he has since left the universe to evolve according to them and does not intervene in it. But how did he choose the initial state or configuration of the universe? What were the "boundary conditions" at the beginning of time? One possible answer is to say that God chose the initial configuration of the universe for reasons that we cannot hope to understand. This would certainly have been within the power of an omnipotent being, but if he had started it off in such an incomprehensible way, why did he choose to let it evolve according to laws that we could understand? The whole history of science has been the gradual realization that events do not happen in an arbitrary manner, but that they reflect a certain underlying order, which may or may not be divinely inspired. It would be only natural to suppose that this order should apply not only to the laws, but also to the conditions at boundary of space-time that specify the initial state of the universe.[3]

The Catholic Church believes that the divine nature, or God, created *everything* in His own wisdom and way. But then, isn't that view contradicted by the prevailing scientific theory? If we were to take the biblical account at face value, the answer would be yes, there is a contradiction. However, we must also consider that the biblical story of creation was formulated by people who were merely trying to make sense out of what they observed in

---

http://catholiceducation.org/articles/science/sc0022.html (accessed August 19, 2005).

3 Stephen W. Hawking. *A Brief History of Time Updated and Expanded Tenth Anniversary Edition.* New York:Bantam Books. 1996. p. 126–127.

the world around them with little or no science to go on.

As our knowledge has grown, so has our theology and understanding. The first book of the Bible, Genesis, states that on the first day, God created the heavens, the earth, day, and night. On the second day, He organized the earth, separating the water and the land. And on the fourth day, He created the sun, stars, and moon. But that account just doesn't make literal sense. Wouldn't the sun need to be created first in order to even have a day and a night?

And this brings me to a crucial point: We need to always use our God-given minds to think about things, and we should never be afraid to question anything. That is, we don't have to believe anything on blind faith. That's why God gave us intelligence, so that we could decide for ourselves what to believe and what to discount. That said, I would venture to say there are three things you must believe unquestioningly.

The first is that you exist. Only you, yourself, can know this. No one else can prove (or disprove) your existence. People can punch you in the stomach or beat you up, but if you say you aren't there, then it's impossible for them to prove otherwise. René Descartes, the French philosopher, said, "I think, therefore, I am," but you must "am" before you can "think" (in other words, don't put Descartes before de horse). Sometimes, after I had been teaching this subject to a class for several weeks, a student would ask, "How do I know that I am here?"

And I would say, "You, bastard, you mean that I have been talking to myself all this time?"

The second thing you must accept on blind faith is your ability to acquire and retain knowledge. Your mind is an amazing instrument that you should constantly use to expand your horizons and learn new things. Remember that you can learn much more by listening than by talking.

The third thing you must believe is what has been called "The Principle of Contradiction." According to the rules of logic, you must define all your terms and, after doing so, you must stick with them. So, if you call a writing utensil filled with ink a "pen," that's fine. But you can't then call the same object a computer.

On a similar note, it's impossible for a thing to be and not be at the same time. That is, either the object in your hand is a pen or it's not. Adherence to this principle is necessary in any logical dialogue. Otherwise, the parties involved could end up talking about two completely different things, wasting everyone's time.

These three beliefs are powerful tools at your disposal. With them, you'll be able to figure out everything else through observation, experimentation, and, above all, reasoning. Faith is a gift, but it doesn't exclude reason. That is what makes a rational being so special. God gave us the gift of intelligence, and we should always be grateful and never take anything for granted. Let us now use that gift to examine various topics.

Protestant	Catholic & Lutheran	Hebrew
1. Thou shalt have no other gods before me.	1. I am the Lord thy God. Thou shalt not have strange gods before *me*.	1. I am the Lord thy God, who brought thee out of the land of Egypt, out of the house of slavery.
2. Thou shalt not make unto thee any graven image, or any likeness *of any thing* that *is* in heaven above, or that *is* in the earth beneath, or that *is* in the water under the earth: Thou shalt not bow down thyself to them, nor serve them; for I the Lord thy God *am* a jealous God, visiting the iniquity of the fathers upon the children unto the third and fourth *generation* of them that hate me; And showing mercy unto thousands of them that love me, and keep my commandments.	2. Thou shalt not take the name of the Lord thy God in vain.	2. Thou shalt have no other gods before Me. Thou shalt not make unto thee a graven image, nor any manner of likeness, of any thing that is in heaven above, or that is in the earth beneath, or that is in the water under the earth; Thou shalt not bow down unto them, nor serve them; for I the Lord thy God am a jealous God, visiting the iniquity of the fathers upon the children unto the third and fourth generation of them that hate Me; And showing mercy unto the thousandth generation of them that love Me and keep My commandments.
3. Thou shalt not take the name of the Lord thy God in vain: for the Lord will not hold him guiltless that taketh his name in vain.	3. Remember thou keep the Sabbath Day.	3. Thou shalt not take the name of the Lord thy God in vain; for the Lord will not hold him guiltless that taketh His name in vain.
4. Remember the sabbath day, to keep it holy. Six days shalt thou labor, and do all thy work: But the seventh day *is* the sabbath of the Lord thy God: *in it* thou shalt not do any work, thou, nor thy son, nor thy daughter, thy manservant, nor thy maidservant, nor thy cattle, nor thy stranger that *is* within thy gates: For *in* six days the Lord made heaven and earth, the sea, and all that in them *is*, and rested the seventh day: wherefore the Lord blessed the sabbath day, and hallowed it.	4. Honor thy Father and thy Mother.	4. Remember the Sabbath day to keep it holy. Six days shalt thou labour, and do all thy work. But the seventh day is the Sabbath in honour of the Lord thy God; on it thou shalt not do any work, neither thou, nor thy son, nor thy daughter, thy manservant nor thy maidservant, nor thy cattle, nor thy stranger that is within thy gates; For in six days the Lord made the heavens and the earth, the sea, and all that is in them, and rested on the seventh day; therefore the Lord blessed the Sabbath day, and hallowed it.
5. Honor thy father and thy mother: that thy days may be long upon the land which the Lord thy God giveth thee.	5. Thou shalt not kill.	5. Honour thy father and thy mother; in order that thy days may be prolonged upon the land which the Lord thy God giveth thee.
6. Thou shalt not kill.	6. Thou shalt not commit adultery.	6. Thou shalt not kill.
7. Thou shalt not commit adultery.	7. Thou shalt not steal.	7. Thou shalt not commit adultery.
8. Thou shalt not steal.	8. Thou shalt not bear false witness against thy neighbor.	8. Thou shalt not steal.
9. Thou shalt not bear false witness against thy neighbor.	9. Thou shalt not covet thy neighbour's wife.	9. Thou shalt not bear false witness against thy neighbor.
10. Thou shalt not covet thy neighbor's house, thou shalt not covet thy neighbor's wife, nor his manservant, nor his maidservant, nor his ox, nor his ass, nor any thing that *is* thy neighbor's.	10. Thou shalt not covet thy neighbour's goods.	10. Thou shalt not covet thy neighbour's house; thou shalt not covet thy neighbour's wife, nor his manservant, nor his maidservant, nor his ox, nor his ass, nor any thing that is thy neighbour's.
King James Bible, issued by the American Bible Society.	Catholic Catechism by Peter Cardinal Gasparri, "published with Ecclesiastical approval" and bearing the imprimatur of Patrick Cardinal Hayes, Archbishop, New York. P.J. Kenedy & Sons, 1932.	Bloch Publishing Company, New York, 1922.

Three different versions of the Ten Commandments.

Figure 3. Graphic layout by Daniel S.H. Mew.

Chapter 2
No One Has a Monopoly on God

Question: What's worse than a self-righteous, fanatical health nut who just found a new diet and workout routine?

Answer: A self-righteous, religious fanatic who just discovered Jesus.

The other day, I was in the elevator on my way to Mass when a woman noticed my Roman collar. She asked, "Have you accepted Jesus as your personal savior?" But before I could answer, she continued on, "Are you saved?"

I then replied, "The only thing I want to be saved from is you!"

But that didn't stop her from continuing, "Would you like to be born-again?"

I chuckled and told her, "I don't think my mom could handle pushing me out a second time."

Far too many born-again Christians want you to know that they are "saved" — and that you should be saved as well. From the number of times I've heard the question, "Have you accepted Jesus as your personal savior?" I'm beginning to think that born-again Christians must have bought some kind of exclusive stock in God. Catholics seldom, if ever, use the expression "personal savior," but when someone does, it means that if he or she were the only person in existence, God would still have come to earth in the form of Jesus Christ for him or her, personally.

What Christian fanatics tend to forget is that, according to the Bible (John 6:43–44), Jesus said, "Stop grumbling among yourselves. People cannot come to me unless the Father who sent me draws them to me; and I will raise them to life on the last day."[4] In other words, God chooses to accept us, and it is arrogant for anyone to think that we need to accept Him first to be saved. Faith is a gift, and if it has not been given to you, then you can't be condemned for not having it. That is simple logic.

But every so many years, the fundamentalist Christians try to impose their beliefs on the rest of us. One of their causes was to keep a copy of the Ten Commandments in our public school classrooms and on government property. The claim was that this wouldn't be favoring one religious belief over another, but do the proponents of that cause even know that there are three distinct sets of commandments? In addition to the Protestant version, there are the Catholic/Lutheran and Hebrew versions. They all essentially say the same things, but not exactly in the same way. The Catholic/Lutheran version, for example, combines the first two commandments into one, and in order to maintain a total of 10, it divides the last commandment into two. So, would the fundamentalist Christians who are so gung ho about displaying the Ten Commandments be willing to let the Catholic/Lutheran or Hebrew version be used instead of the Protestant version? I think not.

Whenever I encounter Christian fanatics, I remind myself not to get sucked into their "Bible Game" by allowing them to spew forth Bible quote after Bible quote to confuse and cloud issues. Even if one's own knowledge of the Bible is exceptional, that kind of dialogue will inevitably just become a pissing contest. And, anyway, the important thing to remember is this: The Bible was never meant to be a weapon against people. Instead, it was intended to be an instrument to tell us of God's presence in the world and in our lives, and to let us know about His unconditional love for each individual person.

But if a complete understanding of God is beyond our

---

[4] Scripture taken from the Good News Translation Catholic Edition – Second Edition, Copyright © 1992, by American Bible Society. Used by permission.

12

human capacity, how can we ever go about finding the truth — and with it, a sense of inner peace? For me, I have found the answer in Jesus, in the Holy Trinity. But not everyone has arrived at that same answer. Yet, regardless of where people are in their understanding of God, we must always remember that God loves everyone equally and that we all can get to heaven if we follow our consciences to the best of our abilities.

Every human person is ultimately seeking happiness. Indeed, that's the primary goal in our lives. But in order to find happiness, we need physical, financial, mental, and spiritual well-being. If any of these is missing, our lives can become difficult and wrought with problems.

Why is your religious or spiritual life so important? Is it because you need to know what the purpose of life is and what happens to you after you die? But if you believe that there is no afterlife, then you don't need to concentrate on that question or spend any of your time or effort on the subject. You could just concentrate on the here and now.

The average American lives to the age of 78. That's not a lot of years (although it's much more than it used to be). Suppose you were given the opportunity to choose how long you will live. Would you then select 90 years, or would you like to live to be over 100? The answer would probably depend on your health, physical abilities, mental capacity, and the amount of money you had.

But no matter how long you live, the afterlife is for eternity. The possibility that death does not mark the end of one's existence has long fascinated humans in practically every generation and culture. For millennia, people have believed in — or at least hoped for — an afterlife of immortality. That's why the ancient Egyptians buried servants along with their royalty. When we are young, we don't give this much thought, but as we age, we think of an afterlife more often, especially when a family member or friend dies.

"Is that all there is?" we ask ourselves. Of course, we shouldn't be preoccupied with death, but wouldn't it be great to know what happens to us after we breathe our last breath?

This is one advantage of our Christian faith. We know that Jesus physically died and rose from the dead, and He said this would happen to us, too.

Other religions have different perspectives on the afterlife, and that's why it's important for people to know the origins of their religious beliefs. Everyone should be aware of the historical beginnings of their church, temple, shrine, or mosque, as well as the basic beliefs, or creed, of their religion.

Some people say they don't like or trust organized religion because it's too controlling. Actually, it should be just the opposite. Religion should set you free from worry and make your life — and death — easier to cope with. Death is a big part of living, and it's important to understand how the two are related. This is why you need to know the origin of your religion, its basic tenets, and where it fits into your life and death.

So now, let me give you a brief background on Catholicism. The Catholic Church is the largest religion in the world, with more than a billion members. It is the original Christian church founded by Jesus Christ, in 33 A.D. The first Catholics were the apostles, who are buried in Catholic churches. (At first, however, the apostles weren't called "Catholic" — a word that means universal — because the religion hadn't yet spread around the known world.) The Roman Catholic and the Greek Orthodox were the original church, but they split in 1000 A.D., not because of religious differences, but because of politics.

The most important difference between the Catholic Church and other Christian faiths, excluding the Orthodox, Lutheran, and Episcopalian churches, is the Holy Eucharist. In the Holy Eucharist, or Holy Communion, Catholics believe that you are actually receiving and eating the body and drinking the blood of Christ.

At the Last Supper, when Jesus said, "This is my body, and this is my blood; eat it," He meant it literally. Of course, the wafers and wine that you receive during Holy Communion do not look like flesh or taste like blood, even though He could

14

have made them appear that way. (But He wouldn't do that to us. It would be too gross!) However, He did say that you are truly receiving His body and His blood, and Catholics believe that anything is possible with God. Jesus commanded us to consume Him so that we might become blood brothers and sisters with one other, as well as with Him.

Think about it: Doesn't it seem like a really beautiful idea what Jesus had in mind when He gave us Holy Communion? Wouldn't you now think twice before doing wrong to your fellow brothers and sisters? If everyone truly believed this, wouldn't there be much less war and hate in our world today? Holy Communion has been celebrated at every Mass on every day since the Last Supper at Jesus' command. The Catholic Church believes that Holy Communion — and not the Bible — is the true link to Jesus.

Actually, the Catholic Church had been around for almost 400 years before the Bible, as we know it, came into existence. In other words, the Church came first, and then the Bible. That is just fact. The Catholic Church put the Bible together and picked out the original 72 books at the Council of Hippo in 393 A.D.

Some Christian fundamentalists might claim that the Bible is the sole rule of faith, but that just doesn't make any sense. These Christians might describe their faith communities as "Bible-based churches." But we, as Catholics, could say that we have a "church-based Bible."

To put it another way, Catholics don't believe something because it's in the Bible, but, rather, our early Catholic forefathers believed certain things, which they then put into books that were later assembled to form the complete Bible.

Contrary to many Christians' use of the Bible as a weapon against others, Catholics view it as an instrument to tell us of God's loving presence in the world and in our life, and to let us know about His unconditional love for each and every individual person.

That's enough about the Catholic Church for now. What about the myriad other religions? On November 11, 1996, the Ann Landers column featured an article entitled, "How Did

Your Religion Begin?" It stated:

- If you are a member of the Jewish faith, your religion was founded by Abraham about 4000 years ago.
- If you are Hindu, your religion developed in India around 1500 B.C.
- If you are Buddhist, your religion split from Hinduism and was founded by Buddha, Prince Siddhartha Gautama of India, about 500 B.C.
- If you are Roman Catholic, Jesus Christ began your religion in the year 33 A.D.
- If you are Islamic, Mohammed started your religion in what is now Saudi Arabia around 600 A.D.
- If you are Eastern Orthodox, your sect separated from Roman Catholicism around 1000 A.D.
- If you are Lutheran, your religion was founded by Martin Luther, an ex-monk in the Catholic Church, in 1517.
- If you belong to the Church of England (Anglican), your religion was founded by King Henry the VIII, in the year 1534, because the Pope would not grant him a divorce with the right to remarry.
- If you are Presbyterian, your religion was founded when John Knox brought the teachings of John Calvin to Scotland in the year 1560.
- If you are Unitarian, your religious group developed in Europe in the 1500s.
- If you are Congregationalist, your religion branched off from Puritanism in the early 1600s in England.
- If you are Baptist, you owe the tenets of your religion to John Smyth, who launched it in Amsterdam in 1607.
- If you are Methodist, your religion was founded by John and Charles Wesley in England in 1744.
- If you are Episcopalian, your religion was brought over from England to the American colonies and formed a separate religion founded by Samuel Seabury in 1789.

16

- If you are Mormon (Latter-day Saints), Joseph Smith started your Church in Palmyra, N.Y., not Salt Lake City (which would have been my guess). The year was 1830.
- If you worship with the Salvation Army (yes, it is a religious group, not just an organization that collects money in kettles on Christmas and serves dinners to the homeless), your sect began with William Booth in London in 1865.
- If you are Christian Scientist, you look at 1879 as the year your religion was founded by Mary Baker Eddy.
- If you are Jehovah's Witness, your religion was founded by Charles Taze Russell in Pennsylvania in the 1870s.
- If you are Pentecostal, your religion was started in the United States in 1901.
- If you are Agnostic, you profess an uncertainty or a skepticism about the existence of God as a Higher Being.
- If you are Atheist, you do not believe in the existence of God or any other Higher Power. This country's best-known atheist, Madalyn Murray O'Hair, has not been seen or heard from in many years. According to her son, she disappeared without a trace.[5]

Indeed, there are many expressions of faith, especially in the United States, where it is estimated that there are more than 30,000 denominations. For example, the Church of Scientology, a religion that confirms the existence of a Supreme Being, but doesn't hold to any faith system or dogma regarding the subject, was founded by L.R. Hubbard in 1954. The Foursquare Gospel Church was founded by Aimee Semple McPherson in Los Angeles. Today, it has hundreds of chapels all over the country known as Hope Chapel. If you belong to

---

[5] Used by permission of Esther P. Lederer Trust and Creators Syndicate Inc.

Unity Church, your religion was founded by Charles and Myrtle Fillmore in Lee Summit, Missouri, in 1880. If you belong to the Calvary Chapel, your religion was founded by Chuck Smith in Costa Mesa, California, in the late 1960s. And the list goes on.

I wonder if this is what Jesus had in mind when He established the Church. But that's what happens when people think they can interpret the Bible themselves. You can see from the proliferation of so many different Bible-based faiths that the Bible is far more complicated than many people think. This can cause great confusion if you do not know the literary form of each book. Not a single book of The New Testament was written until many years after Jesus' death and resurrection. The Bible is the word of God, but not the literal word of Jesus. (After all, nobody was running after Jesus taking down notes of what He was saying.) The Gospels are the ideas of Jesus' words as the writer (the apostles, the evangelists, and so on) understood them.

One thing that sets Christianity and Catholicism apart from all other religions is the belief that God took on our human nature along with His divine nature. Jesus was the only major prophet in the history of the world who claimed to be God. Buddha didn't; Moses didn't; Mohammed didn't; nor did any of the major prophets. Jesus was either lying, misinformed, or insane. Or maybe He was exactly who He said He was: God.

Jesus appears to have been a good, honest man. He didn't seem to try to mislead people. And He certainly wasn't insane. He was highly intelligent, respected by the people, and appeared to have special powers. He changed water into wine.

Okay, I know what you're thinking: Couldn't even an amateur magician perform a trick like that? But Jesus also healed the blind, deaf, and crippled. Could all those people have been suffering from just psychosomatic symptoms? He also brought people back from the dead. Could that have been a trick too? Moreover, Jesus Himself was able to rise from the dead by His own power. He predicted that event and three days after He was put to death, He returned, both physically and spiritually. At first, even His own disciples couldn't believe the miracle and were convinced only after they touched Him and ate a meal with Him.

If there is a God, then surely that Supreme Being would not allow someone like Jesus to come down on earth and allow billions of people to be deceived today. He would never try to test our faith in that manner because He is a just and loving God.

There's something else that makes all Christians unique: the Holy Trinity, which is defined as three persons with one *divine nature*. In chapter 1, I stated that "nature" is what makes something what it is. It's the very essence of that thing. In every generation of Christianity, people have tried to give examples to explain how three persons could be one. Well, they (the trinity) are not actually one person. Rather, they are three distinct beings with the same nature. Consider humanity, for which there are billions of people with the same nature (what we call *human nature*). They are born; they reason; they laugh; they are responsible for their actions; and they die. That is what makes them human.

St. Patrick used the shamrock to explain the Holy Trinity: three petals with one stem, three in one. If you're still confused about the Holy Trinity, you're not alone. I remember hearing the story about St. Augustine, the great theologian from Africa, who was trying to think about a sermon that he would deliver about the Holy Trinity. As he roamed along the seashore, he spotted a young boy digging a hole. The child would run to the ocean and bring some water back to put in the hole. St. Augustine asked, "What are you trying to do?"

The little boy answered, "I am trying to put the ocean in the hole."

St. Augustine said, "That's impossible."

The little boy then told St. Augustine, "It's no more impossible for me to do this than it is for you to explain the Trinity." (What a smart-ass kid!)

As discussed in chapter 1, there are other kinds of nature besides divine nature. There is *human nature* — beings of this

19

type have intelligence; they are born in time and die; they walk; they talk; they can catch a joke; they have free will and are responsible for their actions. There is also *animal nature* — beings of this type are born and die, but they don't have free will. Then there is *inanimate nature* — things of this type (like a rock) aren't born, nor do they die; they just sit there.

Now let me — Father Mac (that is, the smart-ass priest) — give my explanation of the Holy Trinity. We will use the term "God" as the Supreme Intelligence, the Uncreated Creator, the All-Powerful, the All-Knowing, the All-Loving that always was and always will be existing in the eternal now. The three persons (the Holy Trinity) all have that divine nature. We call them God the Father, God the Son (Jesus), and God the Holy Spirit.

We refer to the first person, God the Father, by that name as He represented the qualities of a strong Jewish father of that time — all-caring, all-protecting, the provider of all that was required in life, and head of the family. We attribute creation to God the Father, but all three divine persons were co-creators.

We refer to the second person, God the Son (Jesus), as the redeemer. Jesus came down to earth as our savior. He wanted to let us know that by His taking on a human nature (while still retaining His divine nature), He would be able to understand what it is like being human: how we think and how we feel as a human being, with all the human emotions we experience and temptations we face. We attribute our redemption to God the Son (Jesus), but, again, all three divine persons are responsible for our redemption.

Finally, we refer to the third person, God the Holy Spirit, as the sanctifier. The Holy Spirit gives us the ability to take part in God's life in a special spiritual way. We attribute our sanctity to "God the Spirit" (the Holy Spirit), but remember that all three persons of the Holy Trinity give us the ability to take part in the divine life of the Holy Trinity. With His grace, we are able to be a part of God's life on this earth and in heaven.

Don't worry if you're still a little confused. The concept of

20

the Holy Trinity is not easy to comprehend, but you should always remember this: The Catholic Church believes that God loves everyone equally — every race, every nationality, and every creed. Jesus came into the world for *everyone*, even those who didn't believe in Him — or even know of Him. Furthermore, God created you as a special individual. He put you in this time and place to share your uniqueness with the people around you. No one before or after you will be exactly like you. You are a special individual and are the most important person in the world.

GODISNOWHERE

ORIGINALBIBLEWASHANDWRITTENIN
UNCIALWRITINGTHISTYPEOFWRITING
CONSISTEDOFCAPITALLETTERSWITHNO
CONNECTIONBETWEENTHELETTERSNO
SPACESBETWEENTHEWORDSOR
SENTENCESNOPERIODSORCOMAS
ANDNOCHAPTERSORVERSESUNLESS
THETRANSCRIBERKNEWWHATTHE
AUTHORINTENDEDTHEYHADTOGUESS
ASTOITSMEANING

UNCIAL WRITING WAS
USED UNTIL 800 AD FOLLOWING THIS
WAS CURSIVE WRITING THAT WAS HAND
WRITTEN WITH CAPITOL LETTERS AT THE
BEGINNING OF SENTENCES LETTER JOINED
AND SPACES BETWEEN WORDS

Figure 4. Graphic layout by Daniel S.H. Mew.

Greek Uncial Script (from codex Sinaiticus, 4th century).
Actual width of each column approximately 2.25 in.

Figure 5. Graphic layout by Brian Lee Sackett.

Chapter 3

Don't Worship Any Book, Not Even the Bible

What is the Bible anyway? Is it a book? The short answer is no. Actually, the Bible is a miniature library with many different types of literature. The Bible is the *inspired* word of God, but not His *literal* word. Nobody (including any of the other authors of the various books of the Scriptures) was running behind Jesus and the prophets with tape recorders or notepads and asking, "Could You please repeat that?"

Okay, so where did the Bible come from? It was put together by the Catholic Church in 393 A.D. at the Council of Hippo. Some of the writings were holy (that is, devoted entirely to God or to the work of God), while others weren't. The Catholic Church had the task of deciding which ones contained the history of salvation, not only with regard to Christians. In fact, the Old Testament deals with God's revelation to the Jewish community, their laws, and the prophesies of the Messiah coming into the world. The New Testament foretells the birth of the Messiah and describes Jesus' birth, life, crucifixion, death, and resurrection. The remaining books of the New Testament talk about the early days of Christianity, the establishing of the Catholic Church, and the fate of humanity in the near future. At the Council of Carthage in 397 A.D., the 72 books of the Old and New Testaments were reconfirmed as being "inspired" — that is, influenced, moved, or guided by God.

It was not until my eighth-grade year that I realized that more than a quarter of the words spoken at Mass came directly from the Bible, including the gospels and epistles that are read.

I also didn't know that if a Catholic attended daily Mass for three years in a row, he or she would have heard the entire Bible from cover to cover. I believe that one of the greatest kept secrets in the world is that the Catholic Church was teaching and preaching the word of Jesus nine years before a single word of the New Testament was ever written and almost 67 years before the New Testament was completed!

We, as Catholics, are constantly being asked by fundamentalist Protestants, "Do Catholics belong to a Bible-based church?"

And our answer is, "No! Catholics have a church-based Bible." In chapter 2, we talked about the difference between a Bible-based church and a church-based Bible. The Catholic Church came first, and out of the Church came the writings of the Bible.

Actually, Jesus never wrote any Scripture, nor did He tell the apostles to write. But He did command them to go out into the entire world and preach the Gospel. So, the apostles did it by preaching the good news of Jesus. But as eleven of the apostles were being martyred for their belief in Jesus' divinity (only the apostle John died of natural causes), the followers of Jesus that remained realized that the many things Jesus said and did would be forgotten (Jesus' complete life, death, and resurrection). So, after a short period of time, they began to write down all that they could remember.

Mark and Luke never knew Jesus personally, and the Gospels of Matthew and John were probably written by their followers (as it says in John 21:24). But this doesn't mean that the Scriptures were not inspired by God.

Of course, the more times that something is passed on, the more likely that the message begins to stray from the source and become distorted. But although this could happen to the details of a statement, the essential truth of something that is very important will tend to live on.

For example, if someone said, "As soon as you are done reading the second sentence of the fifth paragraph of chapter 4 of this book, the book will explode, killing everyone nearby!"

26

then surely you would remember that something terrible will happen if you read chapter 4, although you might forget exactly what sentence in what paragraph would trigger the explosion. (By the way, there's no booby trap in chapter 4 and you should definitely read it in its entirety.)

In other words, if all the copies of the Bible were destroyed, the Catholic Church would still continue to preach the good news of Jesus Christ because of the Church's link to Him from the beginning of its existence in 33 A.D.

Today, people know that there are many translations of the Bible. All you have to do is go to any Borders or Barnes and Nobles store and you will find shelf after shelf of translations of the Bible. But if the Bible is the true and literal word of God, shouldn't there be only one translation or edition? So where did all these versions come from?

If you read the foreword of many translations, you'll learn that they were "translated from the original languages." Note that they don't say "translated from the original *manuscripts*." And the reason for that is simple: There are no original manuscripts in existence. There are some fragments of the Scripture, but no complete copies because many of them were destroyed and those that survived had been written on papyrus or other materials that slowly disintegrated over time.

Nevertheless, it is important to know that all Bibles come from the same source: the original Catholic Bible. Every other Bible is some kind of copy of that original. This fact is crucial because so many people base virtually their entire lives on this book called the Bible. Yet everyone should remember that the Bible is the inspired — but not literal — word of God. In other words, God did not dictate the Bible word-for-word to someone, but He did inspire the general message.

For example, the stories of creation in the book of Genesis are not accurate in a literal sense, especially given our present day's knowledge of the universe. So we accept the Big Bang theory and realize that the six days of creation and the seventh day of rest are symbolic, as the number seven represented goodness or perfection.

Interestingly, Christianity was a thriving religion almost 57 years before the Jewish scholars determined The Hebrew Cannon of the Old Testament and 67 years before people had finished writing the New Testament. The first book ever printed in the history of the world was the Catholic Bible, published in 1450 A.D. by Johann Gutenberg, with its 72 books (45 in the Old Testament and 27 in the New Testament). Before 1534, when the Church of England was founded, there were already 77 editions of the Catholic Bible in seven languages.

Today, most Jews don't realize that two versions of the Jewish Scripture exist: The Septuagint, with 45 books written in Greek, and The Hebrew Cannon, with 38 books (or 39, if the book of Daniel is split into two instead of combined into one) written in Hebrew.

The Old Testament in the Catholic Bible is taken from The Septuagint; it was the Scripture used by Jesus and the apostles. But in 90 A.D., 57 years after the Catholic Church was founded, it was decided that only The Hebrew Cannon, which was written entirely in Hebrew, would be used by the majority of the Jewish faithful. Thereafter, the Jewish scholars rejected The Septuagint because it was written in Greek and many believed that God spoke only Hebrew.

The King James (Protestant) Bible took a similar path, adopting The Hebrew Cannon as its Old Testament, but placing the seven omitted books (which it calls the Apocrypha) at the end of the Old Testament. All Scripture that are quotes from the Old Testament and that appear in the New Testament are actually from the Greek version's Old Testament. In 1611 A.D., the King James Bible was printed with all 72 books, but later, seven of those were completely omitted (Tobias, Judith, Wisdom, Baruch, Ecclesiasticus 1 and 2, and Maccabees), as well as parts of Esther and Daniel. Thus, the King James Bible has 38 books in the Old Testament and 27 in the New Testament.

Many times, born-again Christians have asked me, "Why did Catholics add seven extra books to the Bible?"

And my response is, "Figure out the following math problem: If the original Bible had 72 books and the next version had only 65, what happened?" In other words, the Catholics weren't adding books; the born-agains were subtracting them.

My own personal belief of why the Protestants rejected the seven books that the Catholic Church retained is that the second book of Maccabees 12:43–45 talks about making up for the sins of the dead. To me, this sounds like the Catholic idea of purgatory, or offering Mass for the dead, which is completely contrary to the Protestants' belief and one of the main reasons why Martin Luther broke from Rome. Martin Luther believed that the Bible was the "sole rule of faith and we are saved by Faith alone." But the book of James 2:17 states that, "So it is with faith: if it is alone and includes no action, then it is dead."[6] (Okay, so now I'm engaging in the same "Bible Game" that other fanatics play, and I hate that type of bullshit. Sorry!)

Interestingly, so many people take the Bible literally, accepting additional changes that they didn't even know existed. That is, they aren't even aware that certain words or passages in the King James Version aren't in the older copies of Scripture. The added text has no basis as coming from the original, older translations made before 1611 A.D. For example, the ending of the Lord's Prayer, which some refer to as the "Our Father," contains the following words (Matthew 6:13): "For thine is the kingdom, and the power, and the glory, forever Amen." That sentence is thought to be an addition by a pious monk in the Middle Ages and not words from the oldest copies of the Bible.

My favorite passage, again from the King James Version of the Bible (Acts 9:5), is also thought to be added text: "And he said, Who art thou, Lord? And the Lord said, I am Jesus whom

---

6 Scripture taken from the Good News Translation Catholic Edition – Second Edition, Copyright © 1992, by American Bible Society. Used by permission.

thou persecutest: it is hard for thee to kick against the pricks." Should we take that passage literally, especially when its origin is unknown?

Another important thing to remember is that the Bible was originally written in uncial form. What this means is that the text was written with no punctuation, no difference between upper and lowercase letters, and no spaces (or other distinctions) between words. The resulting ambiguity can easily lead to confusion. Consider the following text: GODISNOWHERE. Some people might say that the sentence is, "God is nowhere," whereas others might claim it states, "God is now here." Obviously, there's a huge difference between both interpretations, and even learned scholars can disagree about the meaning of a particular sentence or verse.

Sometimes, even a seemingly small change can have huge consequences. For instance, all Christian denominations use the following passage from Scripture (John 1:1): "In the beginning was the Word, and the Word was with God, and the Word was God." Those words are found in the King James Bible and in all others that profess their belief in the Holy Trinity: three persons with one divine nature.

The Jehovah's Witness translation of the Bible, however, places an "a" before the last word of the verse, turning the end of the passage into "was a god." Is that version thus saying that there are lesser gods? The Jehovah's Witnesses use that passage to state that Scripture does not talk about the Holy Trinity or about Jesus having divine and human nature (contrary to what Catholics believe). Notice that by changing one word, that sentence has a completely different meaning.

The introduction to the Jehovah's Witness Bible states that the text was rendered from the "original languages," versus from the "original Scriptures." Moreover, none of these changes existed when the Jehovah's Witness Church was founded by Charles Taze Russell in Pennsylvania in 1870. And that was many hundreds of years after the first Catholic Bible was put together. So, how did the Jehovah's Witnesses get their translation that said "a" god?

Also, in the Jehovah's Witness Bible, the introduction (foreword) states that Jehovah's Witnesses depend on "the inspired Word of the most High God" for their everlasting salvation. In contrast, Catholics believe that "we are saved by Jesus (Himself) and not by the Scripture."

Most fundamentalist Christian churches believe that anyone can pick up the Bible, read it, and know exactly what each verse of the Scripture means and what it commands us to do. In 1517, Martin Luther, recognized today as the father of the Protestant movement, at first stated that everyone could read the Scripture and understand its meaning, no matter what level of education they had. But he changed his position a few years later after many people began to disagree with his biblical conclusions and contradict his religious ideas.

Today there are almost 30,000 different Christian denominations in the world, and new ones are springing up every day. That's because people think that the Bible is easy to understand. And this isn't only a Christian phenomenon; it is also occurring in the Jewish, Muslim, and other religious communities.

Almost every church, temple, or mosque has a kind of Bible study in which people sit around and give their opinions without any knowledge of what type of literature is involved. When reading their holy book, they all need to ask these questions: Is it literal or poetry? Is it history or allegory? And so on. It is important to establish such fundamentals before the discussion can begin.

The New Testament (2 Peter 3:16) states, "This is what he says in all his letters when he writes on the subject. There are some difficult things in his letters which ignorant and unstable people explain falsely, as they do with other passages of the Scriptures. So they bring on their own destruction."[7]

To complicate matters, certain passages in Scripture seem to be contradictory. During the Vietnam War, for example, one of the favorite Bible passages that the peace movement would

---

7 Ibid.

31

quote was from Isaiah 2:4, "He will settle disputes among great nations. They will hammer their swords into plows and their spears into pruning knives. Nations will never again go to war, never prepare for battle again."[8]

Protesters of the Vietnam War believed that those words proved that war was against the law of God. Many times after listening to them, I would ask them to read the passage out loud to me so that they could hear for themselves what they were saying. Next, I would have them read another passage out loud from the same Bible from which they had just quoted, using Joel 4:9–10 in the Catholic Bible (or Joel 3:9–10 in the Protestant Bible), "Make this announcement among the nations: 'Prepare for war; call your warriors; gather all your soldiers and march! Hammer the points of your plows into swords and your pruning knives into spears. Even the weak must fight.'"[9] Here, it doesn't seem like war was against the law of God, does it?

In 1965, a musical group called The Birds recorded the song "Turn, Turn, Turn." The lyrics, which were taken from Ecclesiastes 3:1, 8, spoke of an "appointed time for everything" and a time "for every affair under the heavens." The song also talked about a time to love, and a time to hate, and a time for war, and a time for peace. So, which verse should we follow? I am not making fun of the Bible, but you can make it say almost anything you want if you don't take the entire work into consideration. And there are many more examples of Scripture passages that seem to contradict themselves.

But that doesn't seem to bother the growing ranks of literal "fund-a-mentalists." Here is group of individuals who bug me to no end. They are the self-righteous, fundamentalist television evangelists who do a much better job of preaching than I do. (So maybe I'm jealous of their talent? Not!)

They have great music and they always have beautiful

---

8 Ibid.

9 Ibid.

wives, the couples dressing in the latest fashions and adorned in expensive jewelry. They are made up to look like movie stars. (Well, all except for Tammy Faye Baker, "Our Lady of Avon," although, at least, she seems to me like one of the kindest and most understanding of the bunch.)

But what bugs me the most about these self-righteous fundamentalist televangelists is that they are always quoting the Bible (as if every word was meant to be taken literally), all the while trying to give us the impression that they are infallible.

And what really sends me over the edge is that they do not practice what they preach! For instance, 1 Timothy 2:9 says, "I also want the women to be modest and sensible about their clothes and to dress properly; not with fancy hair styles or with gold ornaments or pearls or expensive dresses."[10] Hmm, so much for the stylish hairdos, flashy jewelry, and designer outfits.

Another thing that those televangelists always do is ask for money. Often they try to brainwash you with a quote from the Bible on tithing to urge you to donate 10 percent of your hard-earned income for God's benefit. That idea comes from the Old Testament (Deuteronomy 14:22–27), which implies that the purpose of tithing is to provide food, especially to the poor, although no mention is made of any sacred purpose for the practice (that is, as an offering made for God's benefit). But that doesn't seem to bother the TV evangelists, who are only interested in (your) money for their own personal benefit.

In this day and age, everyone in the United States who pays taxes is tithing, whether he or she likes it or not. But these self-righteous fundamentalist televangelists will claim that taxes don't count because the money doesn't go for the Lord's work. Huh? Don't our taxes help educate the youth, feed the poor, care for the sick and elderly, and perform numerous other social services? Isn't that all part of the Lord's work?

Of course, we never hear those same preachers quote Luke

---

10 Ibid.

18:22, "When Jesus heard this, he said to him, 'There is still one thing you need to do. Sell all you have and give the money to the poor, and you will have riches in heaven; then come and follow me.'"[11] I'd like to see every self-righteous fundamentalist evangelist on TV follow that advice.

But Jesus didn't mean those words literally. Think about it. If you sold everything and donated all that money to the poor, then what would society have? One more poor person! What I think that Jesus really meant is this: Don't be so attached to things as to not share them with others. Remember, Jesus never said "blessed are the poor." Instead, He said "blessed are the poor of spirit."

In other words, He was warning people not to allow themselves to be owned by their material possessions. Jesus would never say that we should always be poor. Of course, sometimes in our lives we might benefit from being poor only so that later we can fully appreciate the things we have. But to be poor our entire lives would be a curse, and why would Jesus want that?

Dietary restrictions are another example of how many people take the Bible literally. Deuteronomy 14:7–8 states that, "But no animals may be eaten unless they have divided hoofs and also chew the cud. You may not eat camels, rabbits, or rock badgers. They must be considered unclean; they chew the cud but do not have divided hoofs. Do not eat pigs. They must be considered unclean; they have divided hoofs but do not chew the cud. Do not eat any of these animals or even touch their dead bodies."[12]

In those days, the restriction on eating pork had more to do with health (namely, the fear of contracting trichinosis) than religion, yet many Jews and people of other faiths still strictly adhere to it.

The main point I'm trying to make is that you don't need to take the Bible literally, no matter how forcefully the TV

---

[11] Ibid.

[12] Ibid.

evangelists tell you to do so. And if you're having trouble understanding anything in the Bible, just remember this: You should never be afraid of God because He loves you unconditionally. He created you in this time and place to share your uniqueness with the people around you. No one before you or after you will be exactly like you, and that's why you are so special.

Furthermore, to be "saved" (or to get to heaven or whatever you want to call it), the bottom line is always the same: You must follow your conscience. Cardinal Joseph Ratzinger (Pope Benedict XVI) speaks of the ultimate tribunal as "one's own conscience," which has a place over every authority and which "must be obeyed before all else, even, if necessary, against the requirement of ecclesiastical authority." He says the way conscience is formed cannot be left out of the question and, in the last resort, conscience is "transcendent . . . beyond the claim of external social groups, even of the official Church."[13]

Amen!

---

13 Cardinal Joseph Ratzinger (Pope Benedict XVI) (Commentary on the Documents of Vatican II, ed. Vorgrimier,1968; on *Gaudium et Spes*," Part 1, Chapter 1).

"DO YOU BELIEVE?"
(I BELIEVE YOU'RE TRYING TO DROWN ME ...!")

Figure 6. Cartoonist: Cliff Wirth

36

Chapter 4
The Eight Sacraments (Part 1)

Whenever I mention the eight sacraments, people try to correct me. "Father," they say, "didn't you make a mistake? Aren't there just seven?"

And I answer that by asking them, "Well, just what is a sacrament anyway?"

The definition I learned as a youth in catechism class was the following: "A sacrament is an outward sign instituted by Jesus to give grace." If this is true, then the first sacrament is the Catholic Church itself, founded by Jesus Christ in 33 A.D. And out of the Church comes the other seven sacraments.

An important thing to remember is that the sacraments do not make us children of God because we already are His children from the moment of our birth. Perhaps this is best explained by Fr. Richard P. McBrien, who, I think is the greatest American theologian of our time. In his book, *Catholicism* (chapter 21, page 794), he states the following:

Thus, everybody does not strictly "need" baptism to become a child of God and an heir of heaven. Every human person, by reason of their birth and of God's universal offer of grace, is already called to be a child of God and an heir of heaven. Catholics are not required to believe that unbaptized infants go to limbo, a state of "natural happiness" but without the vision and company of God. We do not "need" the sacrament of holy order to minister to others. Every person, by his or her graced humanity, is called and empowered to minister to others. We do not "need" the sacrament of matrimony to commit ourselves to another for life. And so on. The sacraments signify,

37

celebrate, and effect what God is, in a sense, already doing everywhere and for all. But the sacraments also mandate and equip specific members of the human community, i.e., disciples of Jesus Christ, to be the corporate sign and instrument of God's presence and saving activity in Christ.[14]

The Church is here to remind everyone of God's unconditional love for all of us and to remind us that Jesus is not a bogeyman. And if God thought enough of us for Jesus to assume our humanity (with all its experiences) along with his divinity, then He loves us completely.

Of the different sacraments, three can be received only once because they are permanent. We use the expression, "They put an indelible mark on our soul." They become a permanent part of our spiritual lives and stay with us forever. So, for example, when a person has been baptized (one of the sacraments) into any Christian denomination, "In the name of the Father, and of the Son, and of the Holy Spirit," the baptism is recognized as true and valid by the Catholic Church. That is, if you've been baptized in the Episcopal Church and you convert to Catholicism, you cannot be rebaptized in the Catholic Church. Once you are baptized, it is permanent. (The other two sacraments that can be received only once are holy orders, or priesthood, and confirmation, which is so closely linked with baptism that the two almost seem like one sacrament, but they are separate.)

Keep this in mind as you read on: Every sacrament is here to reassure us, beyond a shadow of a doubt, that God loves us unconditionally. He knows us better than we know ourselves and He loves us, so we never have to fear Him because His love is unconditional.

---

[14] Richard P. McBrien. *Catholicism*. New York:HarperCollins Publishers. 1994. p.794.

Baptism

People often list baptism (for the forgiveness of original sin, which we all inherit from our first human ancestors, as symbolized by the story of Adam and Eve) as the first sacrament, but two other sacraments also exist for the forgiveness of sin: confession, or the sacrament of reconciliation, and last rites, or the sacrament of the sick (formerly called extreme unction).

Baptism reminds me of the story of a young man who decided to "accept Jesus as his personal savior." This young man asked a preacher to baptize him. The custom of that particular denomination was baptism by immersion, and so, the preacher took the young man down to the river. After they entered the water, the preacher grabbed the young man by the shoulders and preceded to push him under the water.

When the young man came up for air, the preacher asked him, "Do you believe?"

And the young man said, "I do believe." And so the preacher pushed him under the water a second time.

As the young man came up again, the preacher repeated, "Do you believe?"

And the young man said, "I do believe."

A third time, the preacher pushed the young man under the water and as he came up, the preacher asked, "Do you believe?"

And the young man said, "I do believe!"

Then the preacher asked, "What do you believe?"

And the young man replied, "I believe that you are trying to drown me, you bastard!"

People often think that baptism is an initiation into the Church, but it's more than just that. When you are baptized, you enter the life of Christ — His complete life — and you become a brother or sister to Him. Each and every person who has been baptized is a member of His Christian family.

Many people will claim that baptism is necessary for salvation, and they might quote Scripture (Matthew 28:19–20):

"Go, then, to all peoples everywhere and make them my disciples: baptize them in the name of the Father, the Son, and the Holy Spirit, and teach them to obey everything I have commanded you. And I will be with you always, to the end of the age."[15]

Moreover, many Christian denominations believe that, to be baptized, you must be completely immersed in water. That is, the water must cover your complete body, from head to toe. Those denominations justify this by referring to a Scripture quote from Matthew 3:16: "As soon as Jesus was baptized, he came out of the water."[16] But I hardly think that God would screw you out of heaven for a few buckets of water, one way or the other.

The Catholic Church has always taught that there are three types of baptism. The first is baptism of water, which is the most common type and the one that most people are familiar with. Water is poured on the head of the person, or the person is immersed in the water. At the same time, the person performing the baptism says, "I baptize you in the name of the Father, and of the Son, and of the Holy Spirit, Amen."

The second is called baptism of blood. This is for people who suffer death for the sake of the faith without receiving formal baptism. The early martyrs who gave their lives for the faith by being thrown to lions, crucified, or subjected to some other cruel death would have received the baptism of blood.

The third type is called baptism of desire. To understand this form of baptism, remember that Jesus Christ loves all human beings. He died for us and wishes for all of us to be saved. The Catholic Church believes that the Holy Spirit offers *everyone* the opportunity of being partakers of the paschal mystery of Christ. This means that when we die, we can all go to heaven and be with God and with one another. So, if we

---

[15] Scripture taken from the Good News Translation Catholic Edition – Second Edition, Copyright © 1992, by American Bible Society. Used by permission.

[16] Ibid.

have the desire to always seek the truth in life and to follow the will of God according to our conscience, then we will be with Him in heaven.

Many people, including some Catholics, might never have heard of baptism of desire, but it is stated in the new "Catechism of the Catholic Church" (article 1,260): "Since Christ died for all, and since all men in fact are called to one and the same destiny, which is divine, we must hold that the Holy Spirit offers all the possibility of being made partakers, in a way known to God, of the paschal mystery." Thus, not only can people of other religions be saved, but also those who don't even believe in God. That's because faith is a gift, and if you aren't given that gift, then you can't be condemned for not having it.

When I lived in Hawaii, some friends of mine who had become born-again Christians were told that their parents, who were Buddhists, wouldn't get to heaven if they didn't accept Jesus as their personal savior. That really infuriated me. So I would ask my friends, "Do you mean to tell me that your parents, who raised you and are good, honest people, won't be going to heaven? If that's the case, then God is not a just God." And that is why I strongly believe in the Catholic concept of baptism of desire, because I do not believe that anyone should be condemned for not having received the gift of faith.

"The line forms at the rear, buddy!"

Figure 7. Cartoonist Cliff Wirth.

Confession

Confession is sometimes called penance, or the sacrament of reconciliation. It is one of the greatest gifts that Jesus gave us. As we know, only God can forgive sin, and Jesus wanted to share this power with us. In confession, we as humans can hear (from our priest) that God forgives us our sins. This practice has its origins in John 20:19–23:

It was late that Sunday evening, and the disciples were gathered together behind locked doors, because they were afraid of the Jewish authorities. Then Jesus came and stood among them. "Peace be with you," he said. After saying this, he showed them his hands and his side. The disciples were filled with joy at seeing the Lord. Jesus said to them again, "Peace be with you. As the Father sent me, so I send you." Then he breathed on them and said, "Receive the Holy Spirit. If you forgive people's sins, they are forgiven; if you do not forgive them, they are not forgiven."[17]

Thus, Jesus bestowed upon the apostles the special power to forgive — or to not forgive — sin as His representative. Note that if Jesus had just told the apostles to forgive people's sins, then it would have been real simple, but He also gave the power *not* to forgive a sin. This is why you have to tell your sins to a priest so that he can make a judgment about them, and that's the origin of confession, or the sacrament of reconciliation. The only unforgivable sin is when you're not sorry for committing a sin, and you make no attempt to stop committing it again.

During the first six centuries of the Church, you could only go to confession once in your lifetime, after baptism (and only for a serious sin such as murder, apostasy, heresy, or adultery). But during the 7th century, people began to ask, "What if I screw up twice after baptism?" And so, they were allowed to

---

[17] Ibid.

go twice. Then the Irish monks got involved (with all their piety), and regular confession became the norm. It got so complicated that penitential books were issued with every sin listed, along with the "proper" type of penance prescribed.

When I was growing up, confession took place in a tiny room like a closet. The priest sat in an adjacent room behind a wall with a small opening covered with a screen. The Church made the confession room very dark so that the priest couldn't see you, and you could remain anonymous. It was all very spooky and mysterious to me, and I'll never forget my first confession. I was seven years old, and I remember going into the dark room, then hearing someone say through the screen, "Yes, my child, is this your first confession?" The voice was so deep and booming that I actually thought God Himself was speaking to me, and I got so scared that I wetted my pants. Thus began my first experience with the sacrament of reconciliation.

In the past, not only were you supposed to go to confession every week, you also had to say how long it was since your last session and then you had to recount the number of times you had committed each type of sin. For me, all of that was too difficult to keep track of, so I would just make up the numbers and then change them around the following time. Once, though, I told the priest that I didn't have any sins for that week, and he told me that that was "a sin of pride."

What a jerk! I thought to myself. "So, it's a sin not to sin?" I guess I just couldn't win on that one, so I said, "I'll try harder to sin next week!"

Today, the sacrament of reconciliation is just as special and valid as it was when Jesus instituted it in 33 A.D. According to the Catholic Church, though, confession is only necessary once a year if serious (or mortal) sin is present, and you — and only you — know when you need to receive penance.

Of course, the best thing to do when you've committed a serious sin is to go to confession immediately. But the Church understands that you might initially be too embarrassed or ashamed to do that, so it encourages you to go to confession within the year.

44

We can also go to God directly anytime for forgiveness, but sometimes we want to be reassured in audible words, as we might feel terrible about something we've done. And that's when we can turn to a priest because we know that he's been given the power by Jesus to hear us out.

Some people still claim that you should go to confession weekly because then you get "special grace." Well, to me that's not confession; that's just "grace grabbing."

I would like to tell you a joke about confession, but I can't. As a priest, I've always been warned not to make any jokes about the subject because people might think that I was revealing something I had actually heard in confession. All priests must abide by "The Seal of Confession" — we can never disclose anything that we hear in confession even if we could lose our lives to protect that confidentiality. Breaking this seal would be one of the worst acts that a priest could commit because then, nobody would trust him again. And the only way he could ever be forgiven is directly from the Vatican.

To appreciate the importance of The Seal of Confession, priests are given the following hypothetical example: A group of Knights of Columbus had scheduled a surprise speaker to give a talk at their convention. Well, the mystery person was late so they asked the local priest to say a few words. The priest began by talking about his priesthood of 30 years and about how much he loved what he did. He described how interesting his life had been, and to illustrate that point, he told the audience that the very first confession he heard was by someone who had committed a murder. *No!*

When he finished his talk, he sat down and, just then, the mystery speaker arrived. It was a famous senator who, as he began addressing the crowd, recognized the local priest sitting just a few seats away. So the senator turned toward the priest and said out loud over the microphone, "Hi, Father, do you know that I was the first person to ever go to confession to you?" So you see how careful priests have to be.

45

Confirmation

Confirmation is the indwelling of the Holy Spirit (the third person of the Holy Trinity). This was not unique to Jesus but to all the people of God's Holy Church, and Jesus promised the gift of confirmation to us on many occasions, which He fulfilled first on Easter Sunday and then more fully on Pentecost, the birthday of the Catholic Church. On that day, the apostles were filled with the Holy Spirit and began proclaiming the word of God. St. Peter stated that this was the "outpouring of the Holy Spirit" and the beginning of the Messianic Age, or the age of the Messiah. Those who heard and believed were baptized and received the Holy Spirit.

Confirmation completes the grace of baptism by filling an individual with the outpouring of the gifts of the Holy Spirit. This seals, or "confirms," the baptized person in union with Jesus Christ. Confirmation helps people to become active members of their parish churches in their worship and acts of charity. Originally, confirmation was conferred as part of baptism, but today, it is more like a rite of passage, akin to an acknowledgment that a person has reached the age of reason.

I was confirmed when I was seven years old, after my first Holy Communion, but the current trend is for people to receive confirmation when they are teenagers (or even later) as a rite of their choosing to become adult Catholics.

Whenever I hear the term, "the gifts of the Holy Spirit," I remember when I was a young priest teaching religion class to girls at a Catholic high school. I asked them, "Does anyone know the names of the gifts of the Holy Spirit?"

One girl gave the name of the first gift, "It's called Fortitude!" So I wrote a big "F" on the blackboard.

Another girl said, "Understanding!" So I printed a big "U."

The next girl said, "Counsel!"

Do you see where this story is going? I proceeded to put a "C" on the blackboard, and then someone else said, "Knowledge!"

As I wrote that letter, one of the nuns entered the room and gasped. "What are you teaching these girls, Father?" she asked.

Still unaware of what I had written, I replied innocently, "the gifts of the Holy Spirit, Sister. Why?" Just then I turned around and looked at the blackboard. To my surprise, there was the four-letter profanity staring at me from the blackboard! By the way, the other gifts of the Holy Spirit are wisdom, piety, and fear of the Lord.

Last Rites

The purpose of last rites (formerly called "extreme unction" and currently referred to as the "sacrament of the sick") is to ask God for physical and spiritual recovery. It pertains not only to recovery of the body and mind (if that is God's will), but also to forgiveness of sin and healing of the soul. Its origin is found in the book of James 5:13–15:

Are any among you in trouble? They should pray. Are any among you happy? They should sing praises. Are any among you sick? They should send for the church elders, who will pray for them and rub olive oil on them in the name of the Lord. This prayer made in faith will heal the sick; the Lord will restore them to health, and the sins they have committed will be forgiven.[18]

When I was stationed in Vietnam during the war, soldiers who were hurt or wounded would request their last rites, no matter what their religious affiliation. I would often ask them, "Are you Catholic?" and they would say, "No, but just in case it will help me." Many young soldiers who were seriously injured but eventually recovered would later tell me that the sacrament of the sick gave them such peace of mind and soul.

As a priest, the sacrament of last rites along with baptism and confession have given my life special meaning because through them, I can reassure people of God's unconditional

---

18 Ibid.

love, forgiveness, and understanding when they need it the most. I'll never forget an incident in an army hospital when I was visiting a patient who was very sick. I whispered in his ear, "If you would like to go to confession, then please squeeze my hand."

I felt his squeeze. I then began asking him some basic questions, and he would squeeze my hand in reply. I felt that we were really communicating well when his doctor came into the room and asked, "Father, what are you doing?"

I replied that I was hearing the patient's confession, and the doctor said, "But this man has been dead for over four hours!" I then realized that the squeezes I was feeling were only muscle reactions. I guess I was just an overzealous priest trying to give comfort — something I'm sure God would understand.

In the next chapter, I'll discuss the remaining three sacraments — matrimony, holy orders, and Holy Communion. Again, we should always remember that every sacrament is here to reassure us, beyond any doubt, that God loves us unconditionally. He knows us and loves us better than we know ourselves, and we never have to fear Him because His love is unconditional.

Picture is from *The Child's Bible History*, adapted from the works of J. Schuster and G. Mey, by the Right Rev. Bishop F.J. Knecht, D.D. Translated from German. Illustrated with 46 plates American edition by B. Herder Book Co., St. Louis, Missouri. Copyright 1890 by Joseph Gummersbach.

Figure 8. Graphic layout by Brian Lee Sackett.

Chapter 5
The Eight Sacraments (Part 2)

In the old Baltimore Catechism, the first thing asked was, "Who made me?" And the answer was, "God made me!" Then the second question was, "Why did He make me?" And the answer was, "He made me to know Him, to love Him, and to serve Him in this world and to be happy in the next." Finally, the last question was, "How do we serve Him?" And the answer to that was, "Jesus said the first and greatest commandment was to love God with your whole mind, your whole heart, and your whole soul and to love your neighbor as you love yourself." (Actually, God said you have to love yourself first, and after that, you should love your neighbor.)

One of the hardest things, though, is to define what love is. We talk about love, we sing about it, we read about it, and we see it in the movies, but exactly what is it? My definition is that love is doing what's best for another being, either another person (including one's self) or an animal. My dad would always tell me, "Mackey, you can't love something that can't return that love." So, for example, you can like Krispy Kreme doughnuts, but you can't love them. Moreover, loving another being is an act of the will, whereas liking something is an emotion.

Remember that God's love for us is unconditional and that He loves us more than we love ourselves. That's why He created each of us to be like no one else. And because we are such unique individuals, we all have a special calling that we are drawn toward in life. Our primary calling is our vocation, of which there are four types: the single life, the married life, the religious life, and holy orders (sometimes referred to as the priesthood). Then there are numerous avocations like being a teacher, nurse, doctor, store clerk, farmer, pharmacist, garbage collector, housekeeper, mechanic, laborer, salesperson, chorus girl, waitress, bartender, and so on. Every one of these is important because they all help to make the world go round.

Of the four vocations — the single life, the married life, the religious life, and holy orders — two are sacraments because they deal directly with a person being responsible for other souls. Those two are matrimony and holy orders.

Matrimony

Matrimony, or marriage, occurs when a man and a woman make a permanent commitment to each other for life. The Catholic Church believes that the sacrament of matrimony was blessed by Jesus at the wedding feast of Cana. In the Church's view, the purpose of matrimony is for the procreation and rearing of children, and the mutual love of the couple.

When a baptized man and woman from any Christian denomination marry, they receive the sacrament of matrimony. Before 1917, if a priest wasn't available to perform the ceremony, then a Catholic couple could get married before any witness. In such cases, because a priest wasn't present to witness the marriage, the man and woman conferred marriage on each other. This is why Catholics recognize marriages of all other people as valid in the eyes of God, but a couple's union is considered a sacrament only if both the man and woman are baptized Christians. After 1917, Catholic marriages required a priest and two other witnesses. The change was made because people were beginning to move all around the world, and the Church wanted to protect a person from being deceived by a partner who was already married to someone else. Today, a Catholic may receive permission to be married with both a priest and a Protestant minister or rabbi as witnesses.

"Marriage" may seem like semantics to some, but the Catholic Church believes that the sacrament of matrimony can only be conferred by a man and woman who have made this commitment to each other and, if at all possible, have done so for the mutual love of the couple and the procreation of the human race. Here, the Church teaches that *potential* procreation is essential for the sacrament of matrimony. Obviously, if a couple doesn't have children because of age or other physical impossibility, then there's no impediment in receiving the sacrament of matrimony. This is because the couple didn't *deliberately* interfere with conception. However, if the couple *chooses* not to have children, then this union is not recognized as sacrament by the Church. To me, that just doesn't make sense because the Blessed Mother Mary and St. Joseph had no biological children together. In fact, according to tradition, they never even consummated their marriage.

Moreover, matrimony isn't the only way for people to commit themselves to others. In his book, *Catholicism*, Fr. Richard P. McBrien states, "Every person by reason of his or her graced humanity is called and empowered to minister to others. We do not need the Sacrament of Matrimony to commit ourselves to another for life."[19] Thus, many people commit themselves to others because of their love, health issues, and other reasons. Some individuals commit themselves to a group, such as through religious orders.

After my mother was stricken with dementia, I was committed to her until she died at the age of 96. Many people have devoted virtually their entire lives to helping others who are mentally, emotionally, or physically in need. People in the religious life take vows of poverty, chastity, and obedience to serve a congregation. Others live together as friends, helping each other through every crisis and problem in their lives.

I know of many people who live together platonically. These unions could be called domestic partnerships even though the individuals involved aren't necessarily gay. And there are gay partners who have committed themselves to each other. People in these types of relationships are often ostracized and treated unfairly by the Church and some of its

---

19 Richard P. McBrien. *Catholicism*. New York:HarperCollins Publishers. 1994. p. 794.

members. But everyone needs to remember that we are all deserving of the help we need in carrying out our mission or avocation in life, and the sacrament of matrimony is not the only way in which people can commit themselves to each other. Nobody has a right to tell anyone else who that person can't love because Jesus commanded us all to love one another.

Holy Orders

The glossary of the "Catechism of the Catholic Church" defines holy orders as, "The Sacrament of Apostolic Ministry by which the mission entrusted by Christ to his Apostles continues to be exercised in the Church through the laying on of hands. This sacrament has three distinct degrees or 'orders': deacon, priest, and bishop. All three confer a permanent sacramental character."[20] Furthermore, that same work states that, "The ministerial priesthood has the task not only of representing Christ — Head of the Church — before the assembly of the faithful, but also of acting in the name of the whole Church when presenting to God the prayer of the Church, and above all, when offering the Eucharistic sacrifice."[21]

Jesus wanted the Church and the priesthood to continue until the end of time. In Matthew 28:19–20, He states, "Go, then, to all peoples everywhere and make them My disciples: baptize them in the name of the Father, the Son, and of the Holy Spirit, and teach them to obey everything I have commanded you. And I will be with you always, to the end of the age."[22]

---

[20] Excerpt from the English translation of the *Catechism of the Catholic Church* (1536) for the use in the United States of America. Copyright © 1994. United States Catholic Conference Inc. – Liberia Editrice Vaticana. Used with permission.

[21] Ibid, paragraph 1552.

[22] Scripture taken from the Good News Translation Catholic Edition – Second Edition, Copyright © 1992, by American Bible Society. Used by permission.

The New Testament (Acts of the Apostles 1:15–26) tells the story of how, after Judas died, the apostles had to pick someone to take his place. So they prayed, then they drew lots (how Catholic to gamble!) and performed the ritual of ordination, or apostolic succession. This ritual — called, in simpler terms, the "laying on of hands" — has been successively passed down from one generation of priests to the next, from the beginning of the Catholic Church until today. Through the ritual, an ordained Catholic priest is given the power to change bread and wine into the body and blood of Jesus, to forgive sin, and to perform all the sacraments that were passed on from Jesus to the apostles. And so the priesthood, or holy orders, is continued today in the Catholic Church by the laying on of hands, and it will continue until the end of time.

No one is really worthy to receive holy orders, but certain people are chosen by God. It's not because they are more intelligent, more holy, or even because they have great leadership qualities, it's just a mystery. I myself have no idea why I was chosen, over 48 years ago, but I thank God for this great gift, and I'm humbled by it. It's also a mystery why Jesus chose certain men to be His apostles. Of the 12, Peter, the first Pope, was the first to deny he ever knew Jesus. Judas, another apostle, sold Him for 30 pieces of silver, and the rest of the apostles ran away when Jesus got into trouble. (What a bunch of losers!) Even today, many priests aren't really qualified for their vocation. But you should always remember that priests are merely human beings who are trying to be holy, just like you. So don't put your entire faith in the clergy. In other words, sometimes you have to keep the faith in spite of us.

Holy Communion

Holy Communion, or the Eucharist, is the most important sacrament because Catholics believe it is Jesus Himself; it's the real thing! The Eucharist — and not the Bible — is the link to Jesus. It was there since the beginning of the Church, whereas the Bible, as we know it, did not come into existence until almost 400 years later. As I discussed in previous chapters, the Church came first and out of it came the Bible. The Eucharist (Mass) was being celebrated nine years before one word of the New Testament was written and almost 67 years before its completion.

The Eucharist was instituted at the Last Supper, when Jesus took a piece of bread and blessed it, saying, "This is my body." He then took a cup of wine, blessed it, and said, "This is my blood; drink it; do this in memory of me."

Many people will quote the Bible and claim, "Jesus said, 'do this in remembrance of me,' and that He only wanted this to be a symbol." But the language that Jesus spoke was Aramaic, and what He literally meant (in Aramaic) was, "Do this to bring Me back."

Skeptics might claim that the Eucharist can't literally be Jesus' body and blood because it does not look or taste like that. But Jesus didn't make the bread and wine look or taste like His body and blood because if He did, that would be too gross! Instead, He said, "This is my body and blood," and Catholics believe it is the real thing because anything is possible with Jesus. He did this for us so that we would become blood brothers and sisters with Him as well as with each other. Think about it. Isn't that a beautiful thought? Wouldn't you always think twice before doing anyone wrong if you knew that he or she was your sibling?

When I was a kid (which now feels like 100 years ago), my close friends and I had a ritual. We would cut our fingers and rub them together to mix our blood. After that, we believed that we were blood brothers and sisters for life. That's why family relatives feel so close to each other — because they have the same blood. Gang members call each other "bloods" because they want to be a family in a special way. Blood has always been a sign of unity, as evidenced by sayings like, "Blood is thicker than water."

Isn't it brilliant that Jesus thought of Holy Communion as a way of making us all part of His family? Belief in the real physical presence of Jesus in the Eucharist is a gift of faith because Jesus is God-man and because, if Jesus can perform any miracle (like bringing people back from the dead, restoring sight to the blind, making the deaf able to hear and the dumb able to speak, and so on), then surely He can change bread and wine into His body and blood. Of course, cynics will always say, "Prove it," but you can't. It is all based on the gift of faith.

When I was in my first Holy Communion class, the nun told us to make a banner and, being in the first grade, I made a sign that said, "COME PLAY SWALLOW THE LEADER." I did it in all sincerity, but the nun thought I was being a smart-ass and gave me quite a beating. (I still have the scarred knuckles to prove it!).

I find it sad that many Christian denominations have made the Bible the center of their faith, unaware that the greatest gift from Jesus is Holy Communion. Catholics, the Orthodox, Lutherans, Episcopalians, and a few others believe that the Eucharist is really Jesus' body and blood, soul and divinity. But the fact that other religious denominations don't believe that doesn't make them "bad" Christians, just misinformed ones. It's unfortunate they lose out on this great experience.

In the Catholic Church, the Eucharistic celebration is called the Mass. The original Mass was the Last Supper that Jesus partook of with His apostles just before His death. The setting of the Mass today is very different from that. At the Last Supper, Jesus and the apostles reclined on the floor on pillows (like being on a chaise lounge). The table was low to the ground, just a little above the floor, something like a Japanese tea table called *chabudai*. The meal was very informal, with people reading from the Old Testament, and then the following occurred (1 Corinthians11:23–25):

For I received from the Lord the teaching that I passed on to you; that the Lord Jesus, on the night he was betrayed, took a piece of bread, gave thanks to God, broke it, and said, "This is my body, which is for you. Do this in memory of me." In the same way, after the supper he took the cup and said, "This cup is God's new covenant, sealed with my blood. Whenever you drink it, do so in memory of me."[23]

Then they sang a hymn and left. This whole celebration was spoken in Aramaic and Hebrew, but later, people made some minor changes in the Liturgy, including the use of Latin, which was more or less the universal language in those times.

During the Middle Ages, many people lost interest in Mass. The rules were so strict concerning the receiving of Holy Communion that few attended. So to regain public interest, someone in the Church inquired what people were doing when they should have been at Mass. It was then discovered that people were going to the opera, to the court of the king, and to magic shows. So the decision was made that Mass should be made more interesting. Thus, the music was upgraded, almost to entertain people like at an opera. The priest would dress up like a king, and he would face the wall to make the ceremony seem more mysterious. The words of the consecration of the bread were said in Latin: *Hoc est enim corpus meum*, meaning "for this is my body." (But because the priest was facing the wall, the words sounded like, "hocus-pocus," a phrase that is routinely spoken by magicians today, even though many don't even realize that historically, it was used to make fun of the Mass.)

Even with those changes, the Church could do other things to make the Liturgy more accessible and understandable. After all, the Rules of Liturgy should exist to help people, and not the other way around (that is, people helping the rule).

Before the changes of Vatican II, only the priest was permitted to touch the Eucharist with his hands and receive the precious blood (the wine). Lay people couldn't touch but had to receive the Eucharist, and then, too, it was only allowed to be received on the tongue. Most of the time, it would get stuck on the roof of your mouth, and you would spend the entire

---

[23] Scripture taken from the Good News Translation Catholic Edition – Second Edition, Copyright © 1992, by American Bible Society. Used by permission.

Mass trying to pry "Jesus" loose. Jesus was probably yelling, "Help, get Me off the roof of your mouth."

Today, some people still don't think that they are worthy of receiving Jesus in their hands, and they are probably right. But Jesus never said that we had to be worthy. He did, however, command us to eat His flesh and drink His blood.

Many Catholics believe they must go to confession each time before receiving Holy Communion. But the only time that people are obliged to go to confession is when they know for sure that they have committed a mortal sin. A mortal sin is a permanent commitment against God (such as apostasy) or your neighbor (such as murder). The punishment is that the person will go to hell, which is a permanent separation from God.

Remember that in order for people to have free will, they must make a choice: to be out of the presence of God or to be with Him in heaven. At the beginning of Mass when we say the Confiteor, "I confess to you, almighty God, and to my brothers and sisters ..." that is a form of confession and venial sins are forgiven. (A venial sin is not as serious an offense as a mortal sin, but it still hurts ourselves or our neighbors.)

Again, all of the sacraments help us to take part in the life of Jesus, but the Eucharist *is* Jesus. If every person who receives Holy Communion would realize that he or she is physically and spiritually connected to others in Christ, that would change the world. After all, how could you harm your brother and sister in Christ? If we all represented Jesus in the world, then there would be no more war, no more crime, no more prejudice, no more injustice.

But it isn't enough to have this knowledge; you also must live the life that Jesus lived (and continues to live through us). In other words, it's not enough just to be a Christian; you must also practice what you believe and have learned about Jesus.

Regrettably, people have committed many injustices in the name of the Catholic Church, but it is those individuals who have messed things up and not the Church. Pope John Paul II has apologized many times for the sins and injustices committed by these members and leaders of the Church, and he has asked for forgiveness. We all need to do the same when we are guilty of something, and we should always remember that we are members of the body of Christ, physically in Holy Communion and spiritually in the mystical body of Christ.

Who is the most important person in the world? The answer is simple: you are. Why? Because you are a unique individual. No one before or after you was, is, or ever will be exactly like you. God created you in this time and space to share your uniqueness with others. If He thought enough of you to do this, then He must have thought you were — and are — very special. God loves you more than you love yourself, and that's the reason He created you. He gave His life for you, and if you were the only person in the world, He would still be willing to give His life for you. This is what our Protestant brothers and sisters mean when they say, "Jesus is our personal savior." Please remember that each of the sacraments exist to always reassure you of God's unconditional love for us, beyond any shadow of a doubt.

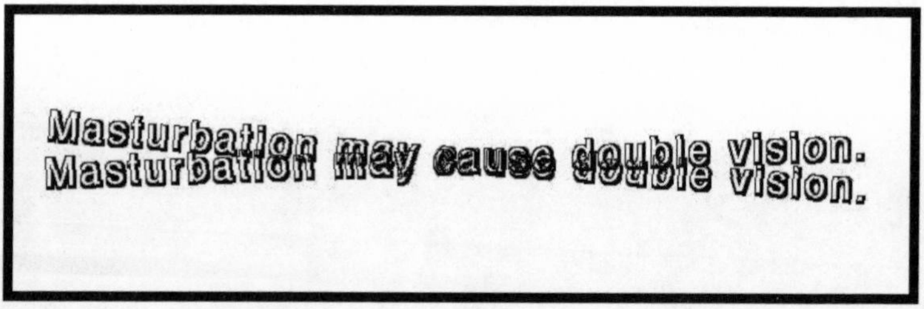

Figure 9. Graphic layout by Brian Lee Sackett.

Chapter 6
Sex and Sexuality

WARNING: THIS SUBJECT MAY BE HAZARDOUS TO YOUR PEACE OF MIND. DO NOT MAKE A JUDGMENT OF CONSCIENCE UNTIL YOU HAVE READ THE ENTIRE CHAPTER.

When I was a young child in grade school, the nuns would tell all the boys that, "It's a mortal sin to put your hands in your pants pockets." Puzzled, I would go home, take off my pants, and spend hours looking in the pockets, wondering what was hidden there that would make something a "mortal sin." And I became so paranoid every time I needed to reach into my pockets.

Sex is the second strongest instinct that a human has, behind the natural drive for self-preservation. But sex is a confusing subject when we are growing up, and it can get even more confusing as we get older. We are told that it is one of the greatest gifts from God, but we aren't supposed to enjoy it. What kind of present is given with the stipulation that the recipient shouldn't take pleasure in it? Some gift! It's like handing candy to a child and then saying, "Don't eat it, except on special occasions. And even then, don't enjoy it!"

There are so many people in the Catholic Church who give us the impression that sex is bad and that God created it as a way to make our lives more difficult, perhaps even to test us. Does this make any sense to you? Well, it doesn't to me. So let's take a closer look at some various issues.

Masturbation

Is masturbation wrong because you are "wasting seed"? But aren't millions of "seeds" released in every ejaculation, so how could countless sperm not be wasted? And is it then okay for women, who do not release seeds, to masturbate? Moreover, is it wrong for a teenage boy to have a wet dream because he'll be wasting seed?

The Catholic Church used to say that a nocturnal emission wasn't sinful "if you were not awake and did not take pleasure in it when it happened." Hey, I thought that wet dreams occurred only when one was asleep. But that's beside the point. What exactly is the sin here? Is it the pleasure? Well, if experiencing pleasure is sinful, then do I need to give up eating Krispy Kreme doughnuts? And what about the monks who invented and produced all those bottles of wine and liqueurs, putting these temptations in people's lives for sinful pleasure? Is eating a delicious meal, listening to beautiful music, or reading a book that moves us a sin? What about taking pleasure in an uplifting liturgical celebration or experiencing any kind of religious or spiritual joy? And is receiving Holy Communion immoral if it brings pleasure? My conscience thinks otherwise.

The "Catechism of the Catholic Church" (paragraph 2352) has this to say on the topic:

By masturbation is to be understood the deliberate stimulation of the genital organs to derive sexual pleasure. Both the Magisterium of the Church, in the course of a constant tradition, and the moral sense of the faithful have been in no doubt and have firmly maintained that masturbation is an intrinsically and a gravely disordered action. The deliberate use of the sexual faculty, for whatever reason, outside of marriage, is essentially contrary to its purpose. For here, sexual pleasure is sought outside of the sexual relationship, which is demanded by the moral order and in which the total meaning of mutual self-giving and human procreation in the context of true love is achieved. (CDF, *Persona Humana* 9)

To form an equitable judgment about the subjects' moral responsibility and to guide pastoral action, one must take into account the affective immaturity, force of acquired habit, conditions of anxiety, or other psychological or social factors that can lessen, if not even reduce to a minimum, moral culpability."(CDF, *Persona Humana* 9)[24]

After reading the above excerpt, you are probably wondering, "What the hell was that all about? Is the Church actually saying that masturbation is an intrinsic and grave disorder?"

When I was in the seminary, I learned that, "if something is universal, then it is natural." Applying that logic, I once asked the Fathers, "As far as we know, masturbation is universal. So then, isn't it natural?" Nobody had a good answer for me and, after that, I wasn't called on for any more questions in the seminary.

Sexual Pleasure versus Procreation

If sexual pleasure is only a reward for procreation, then is it wrong for the elderly to have sex because they can't conceive? And what about when one person in a couple is sterile, or the woman is already pregnant? How can we begin to form any judgments about these people's situations?

By asking these questions, I'm not telling you what you must or must not believe as a Catholic. I am only saying that people might come to different conclusions by following their consciences regarding such situations. Therefore, we must always use our own conscience in determining what's right for us. What may be wrong for one person might be the best

---

[24] Excerpts from the English translation of the *Catechism of the Catholic Church* for the use in the United States of America. Copyright © 1994. United States Catholic Conference Inc. – Liberia Editrice Vaticana. Used with permission.

answer for another.

St. Thomas Aquinas, along with other great theologians, taught that even when a conscience is in error, it must still be obeyed. According to the Catholic Church, in order to follow your conscience, you must devote time to prayer, take into account what the Church teaches, and sincerely think things through to the best of your ability. Then, after following these steps, you are obligated to follow your conscience.

Cardinal Joseph Ratzinger (now Pope Benedict XVI), whom I feel is the best-known theologian of our generation, speaks of one's own conscience as the ultimate tribunal, which trumps every authority and "must be obeyed before all else, even, if necessary, against the requirement of ecclesiastical authority." He says the way conscience is formed must be considered, and in the last resort, our conscience is "transcendent ... beyond the claim of external social groups, even of the official Church."[25]

The "F" Word: Fornication

Fornication is probably the second most common sexual act after masturbation. The "Catechism of the Catholic Church" (paragraph 2353) defines the act in the following way:

Fornication is carnal union between an unmarried man and an unmarried woman. It is gravely contrary to the dignity of persons and of human sexuality, which is naturally ordered to the good of spouses and the generation and education of children. Moreover, it is a grave scandal when there is corruption of the young."[26]

---

[25] Cardinal Joseph Ratzinger (Pope Benedict XVI) (Commentary on the Documents of Vatican ll, ed. Vorgrimier,1968; on *Gaudium et Spes*," Part 1, Chapter 1).

[26] Excerpts from the English translation of the *Catechism of the Catholic Church* for the use in the United States of America.

Is fornication a sin? I want you to notice that the "Catechism of the Catholic Church" seldom uses the word "sin" in referring to sexual matters because sins are so subjective. That is, they are a matter of personal conscience. Therefore, no priest or bishop (or anyone else for that matter) can tell you that you have sinned. We learned in the seminary that "sexual sins" (if they are indeed sins) were the least sinful of all sins. Even so, sex can complicate people's lives and preoccupy their minds more than just about any other actions or thoughts. Sexual urges are the second strongest instinct we have. The only stronger desire is that of self-preservation, or protecting one's life.

Unfortunately, sexual acts can affect not just one's own personal life, but also that of others. This is especially true when conception occurs. Also, if the two people involved in a sexual act have a different idea what that act meant — one thinks it is a permanent commitment, while the other views it as just satisfying a physical need — then this could easily lead to much sorrow, hardship, and even tragedy.

When I was stationed in Vietnam, I went to the orphanages there and saw so many babies fathered by American GIs. The hurt in all those infants' eyes made me ill. I often wondered about the pain those children would suffer in the future. Just because two people have a night of uncommitted, irresponsible, personal involvement, they produced a child — another human being without the opportunities most of us have at birth. (Note: I will discuss birth control and abortion in chapter 7.)

Homosexuality, Gay, Lesbian: The Alternate Lifestyle

When I was a priest stationed at the Cathedral of Our Lady of Peace in Honolulu, Hawaii, I discovered that my church was adjacent to Hotel Street, the red-light district of the city. One night, I was on my way to a sick call and had to pass a nightclub that had a drag show. As I passed the club, two drag queens came out of the club dressed in identical outfits. I said, "Hi, girls. Are you two sisters?"

They noticed my Roman collar and said, "No, Father, we're not even Catholic!"

The subject of homosexuality is very complicated, but I'll do my best to express my views. Already, I may have misled a few of you because, actually, not all drag queens are gay.

First, I'd like to make some general observations about some of the language in the "Catechism of the Catholic Church." By using terms like "grave depravity" and "intrinsically disordered" when discussing homosexuality, not only does the "Catechism" sound offensive at times, but also just plain insensitive and downright mean. I can't imagine how a gay person reading the "Catechism" must feel, especially hearing language like that from a Church that is supposed to teach kindness and tolerance.

However, according to the Vatican document *"Persona Humana,"*[27] from the Sacred Congregation for the Doctrine of Faith (1975), some people are born homosexual and, therefore, did not choose their sexual orientation. It says that some homosexuals are in a "transitory state" and others are of an "innate instinct" or "pathological constitution." When comparing the Church's views on homosexuality, doesn't it seem that gays are faced with a no-win situation, which is hardly fair?

If you are still reading, please don't give up now. Instead, consider this: Before you form your conscience, always remember that God judges you by your own personal conscience, not by the Church's, nor mine, nor your parents', nor society's, nor any priest's.

Many people believe, or perceive, that the Catholic Church has absolutely no use for gays or lesbians, but that's not true. In 1997, the Catholic bishops of the United States published "Always Our Children, a Pastoral Message to Parents of

---

27 Ibid.

68

Homosexual Children, and Suggestions for Pastoral Ministers." This pamphlet states that, "every person has inherent dignity because he or she is created in God's image" and directs parents to love their children unconditionally, even if they don't understand or accept their son's or daughter's sexual orientation. ("Always Our Children" is worth reading in its entirety. The pamphlet can be obtained over the Internet.[28])

Some parents still blame themselves when they learn their child is gay. But no one is to "blame," because people don't get to choose their sexual orientation. According to the "Always Our Children" publication, "There seems to be no single cause of a homosexual orientation." The pamphlet cites the opinion widely held among experts that sexual orientation is a result of multiple factors — genetic, hormonal, and psychological. "Always Our Children" further states that homosexual orientation is generally experienced as a "given," not as something "freely chosen." Thus, the conclusion that could be drawn is that homosexuality by itself cannot be considered sinful, "for morality presumes the freedom to choose."

To me, there's no other alternative: The Catholic community must welcome homosexuals back into our faith community, and I believe that most people in the Church are tolerant. The topic of sex has always been a complicated area for the Church. Nevertheless, homosexuals as well as their parents and other family members deserve a clear and objective view from the Church. They need help to allow themselves to think clearly by trying to understand people of different sexual orientations before condemning and calling them "disordered." People need to examine their own conscience, and I think that more compassion from Rome is deserved by homosexuals and others of alternative lifestyles.

Instead, though, the Church has chosen to alienate. The following excerpt from the "Catechism of the Catholic Church" (paragraph 2357) should be read, not as an infallible

---

28 United States Catholic Conference Inc., Washington D.C. 1997. p.4.

declaration from Rome, but as a statement that is open to review in the future:

Homosexuality refers to relations between men or between women who experience an exclusive or predominant sexual attraction towards persons of the same sex. It has taken a great variety of forms through the centuries and in different cultures. Its psychological genesis remains largely unexplained. Basing itself on Sacred Scripture, which presents homosexual acts as acts of grave depravity (Cf. Gen 19:1–29;Rom 1:24–27;1 Cor 6:10; 1 Tim 1:10.), tradition has always declared that homosexual acts are intrinsically disordered. (CDF, *Persona Humana* 8.) They are contrary to the natural law. They close the sexual act to the gift of life. They do not proceed from a genuine affective and sexual complementarity. Under no circumstances can they be approved."[29]

After reading the above excerpt, remember that your conscience is always supreme. And once again, we need to be reminded what the conscience is: It is that interior voice of a human being, within whose heart the inner law of God is inscribed. Moral conscience is a personal judgment of practical reason about the moral quality of a human action. It moves a person at the appropriate moment to do good and avoid evil, as they see it. A true conscience can be formed by praying, taking into account what the Church says, thinking everything through, and then acting upon that knowledge. An act of conscience is not something that is just done on a whim.

"The Church works slowly" is a phrase that I have often heard. Of course, that's true, but in the meantime, we are driving many gays and lesbians from our Church. At the Bishops Conference of the United States, a statement was

---

[29] Excerpts from the English translation of the *Catechism of the Catholic Church* for the use in the United States of America. Copyright © 1994. United States Catholic Conference Inc. – Liberia Editrice Vaticana. Used with permission.

made to "be open and understanding," yet some bishops are so homophobic that they have gone so far as to refuse Holy Communion to those who wear a rainbow sash to Mass. Now would you consider the actions by those bishops to be sinful? Consider that the "Catechism of the Catholic Church" (paragraph 2358) itself states the following: "Every sign of unjust discrimination in their [homosexual people's] regard should be avoided."[30]

Interestingly, whenever anyone in the Church defends the rights of gays and lesbians, he or she immediately becomes suspect of being homosexual. I'm not sure what the logic of that is. When I defended the rights of prostitutes, no one ever accused me of being one (and if I had been, I surely would have gone broke from lack of customers).

But the situation is not entirely grim. On the bright side, many good, well-educated Catholic priests, bishops, and archbishops have shown much compassion toward homosexuals. We should all especially thank God for Cardinal Roger Mahoney of Los Angeles and Bishop Thomas J. Gumbleton of the Archdiocese of Detroit, who have both accepted the Church's teaching with the same compassion that I imagine Jesus would have. They are intelligent and courageous people who have stood up for the rights of everyone — straights, gays, and lesbians. It simply doesn't matter, and it never should have because people are people. As the Golden Rule states, "Do onto others as you would have them do onto you." The "Catechism of the Catholic Church" (paragraph 2358), too, preaches acceptance and compassion:

The number of men and women who have deep-seated homosexual tendencies is not negligible. This inclination, which is objectively disordered, constitutes for most of them a trial. They must be accepted with respect, compassion, and sensitivity. Every sign of unjust discrimination in their regard should be avoided. These persons are called to fulfill God's

---

[30] Ibid.

will in their lives and, if they are Christians, to unite to the sacrifice of the Lord's Cross the difficulties they may encounter from their condition.[31]

Again, as you think about these things, always remember that God judges you by your own personal conscience, not by the Church's, nor mine, nor your parents', society's, or a priest's, but by your very own conscience.

Marriage and Procreation

I love the Catholic Church and the priesthood. I would never do anything that might undermine its authority. But in order for me to be a good and honest spiritual leader, I constantly need to ask my conscience the questions that the laity ask me. One common question is this: "If the main purpose of marriage is the procreation and education of children and the mutual love of the couple, and if the main purpose of sexual acts is to produce children, then why is it that 'natural family planning' is approved by the Church as a method of controlling the size of their family? Isn't that considered 'wasting the seed'?"

In the past centuries, a couple needed to have many babies in order for them to ensure that they would have a family. At that time, the infant mortality rate was high, and thus, multiple births were for the survival of the family unit.

Today, it's a whole different ball game, and we need to think things through to their logical conclusions. "This is where the Church and Science have to cooperate," as Pope Paul VI requested in his *Encyclical Humanae Vitae*. People now have to ask themselves whether, in this day and age, it's responsible for couples to have as many babies as they are capable of producing. Who will educate, feed, and clothe all these children? Again, people's own conscience should be their guide in deciding just how many babies they should have.

---

[31] Ibid.

Sodomy

The word "sodomy" has a confusing origin. It comes from the city called Sodom, which is found in the Bible, Genesis 19:1–2. The story is about a holy man named Lot and his family, who were visited by two angels one night and so Lot invited them to stay at his home. Before they could settle in for the evening, though, all the men from the town of Sodom came to Lot's home and demanded that he send out the two angels so that everyone could have sex with them. Lot begged the crowd to leave the two angels alone, and to appease the people, he said he would instead send out his two daughters, who were both virgins. The eager men rushed toward the door but the two angels struck them with a blinding light. The angels then informed Lot that the Lord would soon destroy the towns of Sodom and Gomorrah because of the sins of the people who lived there. So Lot left Sodom before it was destroyed.

Now the important question is, why was Sodom destroyed? Some Scripture scholars say it was because of homosexuality, others because of rape, but today, most Scripture scholars say it's because of the extreme inhospitality of the men of Sodom. Yet not knowing exactly what the story means, people have used it for centuries to condemn others, especially homosexuals.

In the past, many Jewish laws were enforced, not because the restricted objects were wrong or sinful in or of themselves, but because they might lead to pain and suffering. Jews were forbidden to eat pork, for example, not because pigs were inherently bad, but because a lack of refrigeration often meant that pork would spoil and harbor harmful pathogens, like the parasite that causes trichinosis.

Similarly, one theory is that homosexuality was condemned in the past purely because of pragmatic reasons. Centuries ago, the survival of the Jewish nation (and other nations) required large populations to defend themselves. But the infant mortality rate was devastatingly high, so couples needed to have a large number of pregnancies for even two children to reach their teens. Thus, at the time many Scriptures were written, population control of any kind was condemned, and this included homosexual acts, masturbation, and any form of birth control. So these restrictions were not based on any moral issues, but as a pure means of survival. Perhaps now, you see that this is a more complicated issue than first meets the eye.

Today, we know that people don't get to choose their sexual orientation, but this was not known in St. Paul's time. I am sure that if he had had this knowledge, he might have written the Scriptures much differently. Jesus Himself never mentioned homosexuality. The truth is that God made each one of us unique, and no one before or after us will ever be the same. We are special because God created us as individuals, and He loves us just the way we are.

Prostitution

When I was a young priest in North Dakota, I was stationed in a railroad town with a red-light district that was located in our parish community. It was my job to do the parish census, which included surveying the houses where the prostitutes lived. Being in my twenties, naive, and innocent (or just stupid), I wondered why all these pretty girls lived together in such old houses. To take the census, I would ask them, "What do you do for a living?"

They would reply, "We are unemployed ... at the present moment." Then they would all laugh hard and poke each other in the ribs and laugh some more. It took me a couple of months to figure out what they really did for a living.

After I got to know them individually (no, no hanky-panky was involved), I realized that they were some of the kindest and most generous people I had ever met. Many had gotten into their profession by some mess that came into their lives. But if ever I needed help for the elderly or I had an emergency with a family, financially or any other way, I could always depend on them for help.

Remember the expression, "Never judge a book by its

74

cover"? Well, never judge people by the way they dress either, even if the clothing is a G-string and pasties. Another appropriate saying here is, "Don't judge people until you've walked a mile in their shoes." That statement is no less true even if the shoes are high heels that have been working the street.

When I first came back from Vietnam, I was stationed in Honolulu at Fort DeRussy. At the time, I lived in a condominium in Waikiki, and every evening, I walked from one end of Kalakaua Avenue to the other for my daily exercise. Frequently, I would be stopped by a "lady of the night" and asked, "Want a date?"

I would always jokingly answer with, "Is there a clergy discount?"

The response would usually be, "What do you mean?"

Smiling, I would say, "I'm a priest!"

And very often, the reply would be, "Hi, Father, I'm Catholic, and I'm a good Catholic."

I sincerely believe that many of those women were. You see, there are many definitions of what it means to be a "good Catholic."

But the "Catechism of the Catholic Church" (paragraph 2355) takes a harder stance:

Prostitution does injury to the dignity of the person who engages in it, reducing the person to an instrument of sexual pleasure. The one who pays sins gravely against himself: he violates the chastity to which his Baptism pledged him and defiles his body, the temple of the Holy Spirit (cf. 1 Cor 6:15–20). Prostitution is a social scourge. It usually involves women, but also men, children, and adolescents (the later two cases involve the added sin of scandal). While it is always gravely sinful to engage in prostitution, the imputability of the offense can be attenuated by destitution, blackmail, or social pressure."[32]

----

[32] Ibid.

Nevertheless, the great theologian St. Thomas Aquinas, in his *"Summa Theologica,"* advocates making prostitution legal as a necessary evil (see volume two, article eleven, page 1222), and he states that the prostitutes may charge for their services (volume two, article five, objection two, page 1459). Perhaps this would be a good idea for the health, safety, and general welfare of the people involved. At any rate, the point is that people can have a great variety of opinions on the subject. The bottom line, though, is always the same. How does prostitution affect the people involved? Remember that the conscience is supreme and you may act on it after praying, thinking things through, taking into account what the Church says, and then making your decision.

Pornography

A young man went to confession and told the priest that he hadn't been to reconciliation for a long time. He then asked the priest to help him examine his conscience. The priest started by asking the young man if he had missed Mass, and the young man replied, "Never."

The priest then asked, "Have you ever stolen anything?" and the man said, "No." Next the priest asked, " Are you bothered by dirty thoughts or by pornography?"

And the young man answered, "Hell no, I enjoy them both!"

Such joking aside, I think it's important to look at what the "Catechism of the Catholic Church" (paragraph 2354) has to say on the topic:

Pornography consists in removing real or simulated sexual acts from the intimacy of the partners in order to display them deliberately to third parties. It offends against chastity because it perverts the conjugal act, the intimate giving of spouses to each other. It does grave injury to the dignity of its participants (actors, vendors, the public), since each one becomes an object of base pleasure and illicit profit for others. It immerses all who are involved in the illusion of a fantasy world. It is a grave offense. Civil authorities should prevent the production and distribution of pornographic materials."[33]

I am curious what scientific research has to say about pornography — for example, does it always cause "grave injury to the dignity to its participants"? One reason I do think pornography can be so harmful is because it creates a fantasy world that cannot be achieved or duplicated in real life. In pornography, the models tend to be unrealistically beautiful, with gorgeous bodies and extra large endowments.

Cheryl Tiegs, the supermodel, once reportedly said that even she wished that she looked like "Cheryl Tiegs" because many ads are airbrushed and touched up to the point that they represent an unattainable ideal.

I am sure that enhancement techniques are used in pornography, not only with photos but also with videos. A pornographer can splice, copy, paste, and repeat a scene as many times as needed. You don't usually have that opportunity in real life. As a result, common people can't compete with the actions in video. This becomes a problem when people who watch a lot of pornography begin to compare their partner's (or their own) endowments, virility, or sexual prowess with that of porno stars. Obviously, the everyday person will rarely measure up (no pun intended).

Sometimes it's difficult to be honest when it comes to sexual matters, but you must make an honest effort to form your conscience. The bottom line is always the same: You must follow your conscience. Once again, Cardinal Joseph Ratzinger (Pope Benedict XVI) speaks of the ultimate tribunal as "one's own conscience," which has a place over every authority and which "must be obeyed before all else, even, if necessary, against the requirement of ecclesiastical authority." Moreover, he states that the way a person's conscience is formed cannot be left out of the equation, and

---

[33] Ibid.

in the last resort, conscience is "transcendent ... beyond the claim of external social groups, even of the official Church."[34]

    To that, I say, "Amen!"

---

[34] Cardinal Joseph Ratzinger (Pope Benedict XVI) (Commentary on the Documents of Vatican ll, ed. Vorgrimier, 1968; on *Gaudium et Spes*," Part 1, Chapter 1).

Figure 10. Graphic layout and digital photograph
by Daniel S.H. Mew.

Chapter 7
Social Issues and Tragedies of Our Time

We live in an age that is vastly different from just a few generations ago. Back then, it was rare to hear people mention — let alone discuss — suicide, sexual abuse, abortion, birth control, and a host of other taboo topics. Today, watch any daytime talk show and you'll hear such subjects discussed in graphic detail. Many of those shows exploit and often trivialize the experiences of people who have suffered tremendous pain. But these topics are important, and they bear serious and thoughtful discussion.

Suicide

Suicide was once considered an act that could never be forgiven. It was a mortal sin, and after death, there was no way to repent for it. It was "automatic damnation to hell." What a tragedy that such beliefs were so widespread. Think of the added suffering they must have brought to not only the individual who committed suicide, but also to that person's family and loved ones who were left behind.

As a pastor, one of my first assignments was to a parish with an adjacent cemetery. On my first day there, I noticed a number of black crosses just outside the cemetery fence. Curiosity instantly struck me, so I inquired what those crosses were for, and someone told me they marked the graves of people who had committed suicide. I was stunned. But after getting over my initial shock, I proceeded the next day to have the fence moved so that these graves would lie within the cemetery. I also had all black crosses painted white, and I publicly apologized the following Sunday to the families of those souls and asked for their forgiveness, not just for myself, but also for the Church.

Ignorance about suicide has caused so much harm and pain. At the time when those individuals were buried, people were not aware that many who committed suicide suffered from depression, a severe mental illness. Instead, they might have known that the strongest instinct of human beings is that of self-preservation, and to go contrary to that was wrong. And the Church at that time was just trying to stop people from taking their own lives, so priests thought that if they told everyone that suicide was a mortal sin, people wouldn't do it. Thank God we have outgrown that ignorance. We now understand how severely debilitating depression can be.

For an act to be a mortal sin, three things are necessary: It must be a grievous matter; it must have been committed after sufficient reflection; and it must occur with full consent of the will. Suicide is indeed a grievous act, but people who are suffering so much from depression that they kill themselves don't have the mental capacity necessary for sufficient reflection, nor do they have complete free will.

For the family and friends left behind after a loved one's suicide, I have a special message for you: It's not your fault because there was nothing you could do. Just because a loved one committed suicide does not mean that the person didn't love or trust you. In fact, the suicide had nothing to do with you, and you will know this when you get to heaven and can talk with that person. I believe that God has a special love for people who have suffered so much from depression that they were driven to suicide, because He's always had such tremendous compassion for the sick.

Sexual and Other Types of Abuse

Today the Catholic Church has been deeply saddened by every case of sexual abuse involving some members of the clergy. Just 20 years ago, no one would have believed that this was ever possible. From all the extensive media coverage, you might begin to think that promiscuity is rampant in the seminaries. But having attended them for over eight years, I can say that's absolutely not the case. Furthermore, contrary to some media accounts, you might be surprised to know that a smaller percentage of Catholic clergy commit acts of sexual abuse than do people in the general population. Regardless, sexual abuse — or any other kind of abuse for that matter — is always wrong and can never be justified.

When I had a parish in Hawaii, I would often deliver a sermon about spousal abuse by showing clips from *Sleeping with the Enemy*. The movie, which stars Julia Roberts, is about a housewife who is married to an abusive man. He demeans, hits, and kicks her, leaving her in a constant state of terror.

After showing the clips, I would ask the congregation, "Do you think that Jesus would want this woman to stay in this relationship?"

To me the answer is obvious, but some people would say, "Father, when she got married, though, didn't she promise that it was for better or for worse?"

Then I would ask them this: "Do you think for one moment that she would have said, 'I do,' to that vow if she had any idea that he would treat her like that?"

Abuse does not have to be sexual or physical. It can also be mental: Someone constantly putting another down, taking away that person's confidence or pride, or ruining his or her reputation.

Michael Trueman, a judge in the Archdiocese of Detroit, quotes the Canon Law (Canon 220) of the Catholic Church as stating, "No one may unlawfully harm the good reputation which a person enjoys or violate the right to protect his or her privacy."[35] Trueman believes that every person has the right to a good reputation, that this is "a natural law written into the human conscience." Furthermore, he says that any "person of goodwill knows not to frustrate the reputation of another" and

---

[35] Pete Vere & Michael Trueman. *Surprise by Canon Law.* Cincinnati:St. Anthony Messenger Press. 2004. chapter 2 article 19 page 17.

reminds people that they only need "to think of Christ's teaching to be wary of criticizing others."[36]

He also quotes Luke 6:41–42: "Why do you look at the speck in your brother's eye, but pay no attention to the log in your own eye? How can you say to you brother, 'Please, brother, let me take that speck out of your eye,' yet cannot even see the log in your own eye? You hypocrite! First take the log out of your own eye, and then you will be able to see clearly to take the speck out of your brother's eye."[37]

There is also such a thing as spiritual abuse. Unfortunately, some bishops, priests, nuns, brothers, and deacons have spiritually bullied the laity by disregarding people's conscience. Many a sincere person has gone to confession, only to have a priest verbally abuse the penitent, stripping that individual of hope and dignity. And there are numerous other examples: A bishop refuses to give Holy Communion to people who wore a rainbow sash in honor of gay pride; a priest denies Holy Communion to people who are pro-choice. Perhaps those clergy have forgotten that Jesus condemned sin, but never the sinner.

So whenever people ask me, "Father, how can divorced people go to Holy Communion?" I tell them, "that is between those individuals and God only." I never have — and never will — refuse Holy Communion to anyone. When you get right down to it, nobody — not even the Pope — is truly worthy to receive the body and blood of Christ. But Jesus didn't say we had to be worthy. He did, though, command us to eat His body and drink His blood so that we could become blood brothers and sisters with Him and with each other.

Abortion

One of the most difficult social issues today is abortion. I know why some women want to obtain an abortion, but what is

---

[36] Ibid.
[37] Ibid.

84

its morality? From the moment of conception, when a sperm unites with an egg, the result is a potential human being. The problem is that neither science nor religion can tell us exactly when the human soul unites with the human body. Therefore, I'm not sure how you can terminate something when you're not certain if it's a human being.

For example, if you were in a room and thought you saw a bear lurking at the door, you might shout, "There's a bear. Shoot it!"

But what if someone else said, "No, that's not a bear. It's a lady wearing a fur coat." Then the logical thing to do would be to ask yourself this: Should I shoot something without first being positive what it is? I don't think that anyone should. And that's why I have to wonder about abortion.

Some people will say that the fetus is part of the mother's body, and that it can't live on its own. That's true, but a child who is five years old also can't live without his mother either. So should any mother be able to terminate the life of a five-year-old child? Of course not.

Other people will claim that abortion is the right of every woman. But I have to question whether an embryo or fetus also has rights, especially when we don't know for sure at what moment that entity becomes a human being. Does that happen at conception, at birth, or somewhere in between?

The issue gets even more complicated when a woman's life is jeopardized by her pregnancy. In such situations, you need to have the complete facts before deciding anything.

In all my years of hospital work, I have never seen anyone struggle with such a decision, because the cases were all pretty cut-and-dry. Say, for example, that a woman has an ectopic pregnancy that threatens her life, so a doctor terminates the pregnancy. The intent was to save the woman's life even though the procedure resulted in the loss of the embryo. But what was the alternative, to let the pregnancy continue, thus endangering not only the woman's life, but also the embryo? What sense does that make?

Many Catholics believe that the Church's view is that, if

the choice is between the life of the mother and that of an unborn child, the child must be saved at all costs. But that's not the case, and in 1951, Pope Pius XII stated so.[38] The obligation is to make every effort to save both lives, but sometimes that can't be done. In such situations, people just have to make the best decision they can after weighing all the facts. Remember that personal conscience is supreme, but you are always responsible for your own actions.

Birth Control

Birth control is a subject that I am actually an authority on because I have practiced it my entire life. Celibacy might be unnatural, but it is approved by the Catholic Church. Almost every man who is ordained into the priesthood in the Roman Catholic Church is required to take the vow of lifetime celibacy. The exceptions are ministers of other Christian denominations who were married before they converted to Catholicism and were then ordained. Priests of the Eastern rite of the Catholic Church who were married before they were ordained are also exempt. Eastern rite Catholics, which include the Byzantine, Armenian, Chaldean, Syrian, Maronite, and Coptic, are under the Pope of Rome, but they have their own Liturgy, or style of celebrating Mass.

Of course, celibacy is not the only form of birth control, which includes everything from pharmaceuticals to surgery. Fr. Richard McBrien summarized this in the original 1980 edition of his book *Catholicism*, Volume II, Part V, page 1050

Summary 2: Birth control, or the conscious regulation of births, is not totally and absolutely rejected by Catholic theology and doctrine. The rhythm method, for example, is an accepted way of avoiding pregnancy. What is at issue, therefore, is contraception by artificial means: e.g., pill, IUD,

---

[38] Pope Pius XII address to the Family Front Congress, November 27, 1951.

foam, condom. The argument between the two opposing sides in the Catholic Church was joined in 1968 with the publication of *"Humanae Vitae,"* the papal encyclical which rejected artificial contraception of every kind.

Summary 7: The reaction to *"Humanae Vitae"* was diverse: all the way from unequivocal acceptance to outright rejection. Many other positions fell somewhere in between: e.g., various statements from national bodies of bishops which emphasized the primacy of conscience and the mercy and forgiveness of God. The Vatican carried forward its traditional teaching on sexual ethics in a declaration on the same subject in 1975.

Summary 8: There are certain Christian values underlying this issue of birth control which must always be taken into account: (1) the goodness of procreation as an expression of mutual love and for the welfare of the human community at large; (2) the sanctity of human life; (3) the personal dignity and welfare of the spouses, their children, and potential children; (4) the inviolability of conscience; (5) the responsibility to act on an informed conscience; (6) the right and the responsibility of the Church to teach on such matters; (7) the duty to take such teachings into account.[39]

In other words, the issue of personal conscience is of paramount importance here. To address that issue, Cardinal Joseph Ratzinger (Pope Benedict XVI) speaks of the ultimate tribunal, "one's own conscience," which has a place over every authority and "must be obeyed before all else ..." He says the way conscience is formed cannot be left out of the question and, in the last resort, conscience is "transcendent . . . beyond the claim of external social groups, even of the official

---

[39] Fr. Richard P. McBrien. *Catholicism*, Volume II, Part V. HarperCollins Publishers. 1980. p.1050.

Church."[40]

Excommunication

God created you in this time and place so that you could share your uniqueness with your family, friends, and everyone else you come to know. This is why you are so very important, even though sometimes you might not feel that way. But you need to realize just how important you are. If you were the only person left on earth, Jesus would still come down to save you because He loves you that much. And if He feels that way about you, then you, too, must remember to always love yourself.

But many people forget to do that, and they might think that they are no longer members of the Catholic Church because of their divorce, use of birth control, sexual orientation, or some other reason. But you can always be a member of the Church if you want to be. Remember this: No one can excommunicate you from the Church; only you can if you violate a major rule, such as having an abortion. The pope, a bishop, or a priest may formally call the law or rule to your attention, but you, alone, make the final decision whether to follow it or not.

And excommunication does not mean that you are damned to hell. It is meant just to urge you to reform your life in some way. Excommunication lasts until you acknowledge your error and ask for forgiveness, or until you change that part of your life.

While I'm on the topic of excommunication, I should clear up a common misconception held by gay Catholics who have forsaken the Church because they mistakenly believe they would be excommunicated for their sexual orientation. Some of them might feel that, to be accepted by the Church, they

---

[40] Cardinal Joseph Ratzinger (Pope Benedict XVI) (Commentary on the Documents of Vatican ll, ed. Vorgrimier,1968; on *Gaudium et Spes*, Part 1, Chapter 1).

would first have to change and become heterosexual. But that's not the case. In one of its documents called *"Personal Humana,"* written by the Sacred Congregation for the Doctrine of Faith, the Church states that a person can be born gay. If that's the case, isn't that what God had intended for that person? And if so, how could that person be excommunicated by the Church?

Remember the bottom line is always the same: Your conscience is supreme. God will judge you by your conscience, not the Church's, or your spouse's, or your family's, or your children's, or your friends', or your neighbors', or anyone else's. Here I need to apologize to anyone who was made to feel that he or she had been judged by a member of the Church and whose hope and faith had been taken away by that person. The truth is that only God can judge you, and you will not go wrong if you always follow your conscience.

Divorce

Many people think they are no longer members of the Church because they are divorced. They believe that they've been excommunicated and cannot receive Holy Communion. That was true before Vatican II, when people needed to have permission from the church for a civil divorce, but this law is no longer enforced. If you are divorced and have remarried, though, that's another story. Either you should seek an annulment or use the "internal forum" solution. But I'm getting ahead of myself. The first and real question is: What is marriage?

As we discussed in chapter 5, a marriage occurs when a man and a woman make a permanent commitment to each other for life. The initial idea of marriage comes from the first book of the Old Testament (Genesis 2:18): "Then the Lord

God said, 'It is not good for man to be alone.'"[41] Then Genesis 2:22 states, "He formed a woman out of the rib ..."[42] and Genesis 2:24 explains, "That is why man leaves his father and mother and is united with his wife, and they become one."[43] The idea of marriage can also be found in the New Testament (Matt 19:3–6):

"Some Pharisees came to him and tried to trap him by asking, 'Does our law allow a man to divorce his wife for whatever reason he wishes?' Jesus answered, 'Haven't you read the Scripture that says that in the beginning the Creator made people male and female?' And God said, 'For this reason a man will leave his father and mother and unite with his wife, and the two will become one.' So they are no longer two, but one.' No human being must separate, then, what God has joined together."[44]

We used to think that marriage was easy: All you had to do was to say the magic words, " I do," and then live happily thereafter. But marriage isn't that simple. First, you have to know, or have some idea, what you are saying "I do" to. If you knew that your partner was going to be unfaithful, abusive, or suffer a major mental illness like schizophrenia, would you be so quick to mutter the words, "I do"?

Today, Catholics who are divorced and haven't remarried are always welcomed in the Church and encouraged to receive Holy Communion. If they are divorced and want to remarry, they should apply for an annulment or consider the "internal forum" solution, which I'll discuss in the next section. Neither of these options should be taken lightly.

---

[41] Scripture taken from the Good News Translation Catholic Edition – Second Edition, Copyright © 1992, by American Bible Society. Used by permission.

[42] Ibid.

[43] Ibid.

[44] Ibid.

Annulment

Sometimes when a marriage fails, the two people ask themselves, "Was this really a marriage?" or, "Was there something crucial I should have known before I took my vows?" This is when a couple may decide on a civil divorce, and many people might also consider obtaining an annulment from the Catholic Church.

An annulment is an official declaration that a marriage never existed in the first place. Technically, an annulment is not a divorce, as the Catholic Church does not grant divorces. Marriages can be annulled for a variety of reasons, including a lack of partnership in conjugal life or the absence of conjugal love. Annulments can also be granted because of a person's psychopathic personality, sociopathic behavior, schizophrenia, affective immaturity, moral impotence, lack of interpersonal communication, and so on. If the couple has had children, an annulment doesn't make them illegitimate, as there are no illegitimate children, only illegitimate parents.

But what happens to people who can't obtain an annulment? Are they trapped for the rest of their lives? The answer is no, because there is an alternative: the "internal forum" solution. According to Richard P. McBrien in his book, *Catholicism* (page 862), the Marriage Tribunal, or court, of the diocese or of the Holy See is referred to as the "external forum." Its proceedings are public and decisions are rendered in the open. But it's not always possible to find adequate public reasons justifying an annulment decree. In such difficult cases, the Church is still committed to providing a caring and compassionate ministry toward those who are in stable and responsible second marriages. So, when a Catholic has, after prayerful consultation, decided to remarry or to remain in his or her present second marriage, the individual may possibly be readmitted to the Church's sacramental life, assuming that no grave scandal is involved. This decision — referred to as the "internal forum" solution — is made based on theological opinion and pastoral practice. Individuals who are granted either an annulment or "internal forum" solution must still honor their moral and legal obligations remaining from their prior marriage.[45]

Social Justice

Being raised in Detroit, the auto capital of the world, I've always considered the right to form a union as essential. Long ago, before unions were established, if you worked on an assembly line and got sick or fainted, you were immediately hauled off the line, your time card was punched for you, and then you were fired. This after you had been working nonstop for 12 hours without a break to eat or use the restroom. The company believed that it owned you, and that's how the labor strikes started and why they often turned violent. The country owes a lot to unions as they helped establish the obligation of companies to provide employees with just wages and decent working conditions.

When I was a student at a Catholic High School in the 1940s, we learned about the Church's teaching on social justice. There were two encyclicals in particular that were emphasized: *Rerum Novarum,* "On the Condition of the Working Man," written in 1891 by Pope Leo XIII; and *Quadragesim Anno,* "Reconstructing the Social Order," written in 1931. Both deal with issues of the role of the government in society and in the economy, the right of laborers to organize, and the principle of a just wage. These two encyclicals, which provide a Christian critique of both capitalism and socialism, have taught people a lot. In fact, they helped change the working conditions, both for employees and employers, persuading society of the concept of "a just wage for a just day's work."

If you have ever worked for the Catholic Church, then I know what you're thinking: If bishops, priests, and nuns have

---

[45] Richard P. McBrien. *Catholicism.* New York: HarperCollins Publishers.1994. p. 862.

read these encyclicals, then why are the teachers in Catholic schools, the church organists, and all other employees of the Church getting such low wages, often without any benefits or pension plans?

I know the pat answer: The Church is a nonprofit organization. True, but that shouldn't be an excuse for social injustice. If parishioners want the Church's services, then they must pay for them. I know that doesn't sound great, but what's right is right, and no one should be taken for granted on this.

Years ago, I complained to a bishop that priests weren't making enough money. At the time, our wages topped a dollar a day. That's just $365 a year! The bishop told me, "But you get room and board; therefore, you should be able to save some each month." And then he said, "You didn't go into the priesthood for the money, did you?"

That really pissed me off, and I told him that if I didn't love the priesthood, I wouldn't put up with his crap for a million dollars. Sometimes bishops and other Church officials can be real bastards, not just to parishioners, but to other clergy as well.

Teachers at Catholic schools have often gotten the same treatment. The administration will say, "Aren't you doing this because you are dedicated to Jesus?" But you can't eat and pay your bills with dedication. Unfortunately, Church officials and administrators often forget what Jesus said: "Workers should be given their pay."[46]

Because of the current shortage of priests, one topic that has generated a great deal of attention today is whether women should be ordained to the priesthood. If you've ever asked that question, you might have received the pat answer that Jesus ordained only men. Well, that's true, but He also ordained only Jewish men. Because of that, should I have been denied the priesthood simply because I'm Irish? So whenever people ask me whether women should be allowed to become priests, I always answer, "Why not?" After all,

---

[46] Good News Bible (Luke 10, 7).

what do priests do at the altar that women can't do?

Racial Discrimination

When I was in my early 20s, I traveled for the first time to the South. It was my first encounter with blatant racial discrimination. Never before had I witnessed segregation. Not only were the restrooms marked "for whites only" or "for blacks only," but also the drinking fountains and lunch counters were designated that way.

During my trip, I stayed with the family of one of my classmates. They were very rich and had what they called at the time "colored" servants. When it was supper time, the black help would serve us and then go out to the back porch to eat their meal. I was shocked. I told my friend that I wanted to join the servants to eat on the back steps. But he told me to sit down and not make any waves. "You don't understand," he said. "They know their place." I couldn't believe what was happening, especially because my friend and his family were dedicated Catholics and outstanding people in so many other ways.

Racial discrimination has been rampant for hundreds of years. And it still exists today in the U.S., although to a lesser degree, thanks to heroes like Dr. Martin Luther King, Malcolm X, Rosa Parks, and others. Where was the Catholic Church at that time? Although many Catholic bishops, priests, nuns, and lay people were involved in civil-rights causes, the Church, as a whole, didn't do much to stop the injustices. That just didn't make any sense, especially because of the fact that, during the first 500 years of the Catholic Church, at least three popes were black, and one of the greatest theologians of the Church was St. Augustine of Hippo, whose father was a Roman solider and whose mother was St. Monica, a black woman.

Today the Church is trying to help in certain ways, for example, by its involvement in the inner-city parochial school systems in the U.S. and by dedicating itself to teaching young black students, most of whom are not Catholic. But perhaps more could be done so that we never repeat our past mistakes, not only with respect to blacks, but also with regards to all other racial, ethnic, and religious groups.

War

As a Vietnam veteran with two Bronze Star Medals, I can tell you from personal experience that war is indeed hell. But not everyone wants peace, and some people feel they have the right to take away the rights, property, or possessions of others. So it sometimes becomes necessary to defend yourself or to fight for others who are being oppressed.

During the Vietnam War, I worked with and had contact with thousands of refugees who had fled the North because, among other reasons, they weren't allowed to practice their religion, either Catholicism or Buddhism. My own personal view is that we lost that war militarily, but we won in other ways. After people saw how prosperous we Americans were, both the North and the South Vietnamese realized that material wealth was what they wanted, and they no longer would settle for living in poverty and strife.

Whenever a nation goes to war, people who are opposed to it will quote the Bible, especially Isaiah 2:4: "He will settle disputes among great nations. They will hammer their swords into plows and their spears into pruning knives. Nations will never again go to war, never prepare for battle again."[47] Meanwhile, others in favor of war will quote Joel 3:9–10: "Make this announcement among the nations: 'Prepare for war; call your warriors; gather all your soldiers and march! Hammer the points of your plows into swords and your pruning knives into spears. Even the weak must fight.'"[48] Sometimes it seems like you can justify just about anything by quoting the Bible, if

---

[47] Scripture taken from the Good News Translation Catholic Edition – Second Edition, Copyright © 1992, by American Bible Society. Used by permission.

[48] Ibid.

you look long enough.

The truth is that Jesus was not a pacifist. After all, He used a whip in the temple against a money changer. But Jesus was hardly the type to look for a fight, and He warned that, "He who lives by the sword will die by the sword." Still, Jesus never implied that you shouldn't defend yourself. And sometimes you must fight to help others, especially those who can't defend themselves, all in the name of Christian charity. It's true that Jesus did preach, "Turn the other cheek," but He also didn't say you should become a doormat and let others walk all over you.

Moreover, Jesus didn't seem to be categorically opposed to war. According to Luke 3:14, "Some soldiers also asked him, 'What about us? What are we to do?' He said to them, 'Don't take money from anyone by force or accuse anyone falsely. Be content with your pay.'"[49] Note that Jesus didn't tell the soldiers to quit the army, and others in the Church have come to believe that there is such a thing as a "just war."

Back in the 13th century, St. Thomas Aquinas listed three requirements for a just war: 1) a just cause, 2) legitimate authority, and 3) the right intention. Later, other criteria were added: 4) the last resort, 5) formal declaration of the war, 6) reasonable hope of success, 7) proportion between the good accomplished (or evil avoided) and the evil caused by the war itself, 8) immunity of noncombatants from direct attack, and 9) proportionality of tactics and means to an end.

Nuclear war can't satisfy many of the criteria for a just war. For instance, how can you ensure that civilians won't be harmed? This is why I feel that nuclear war is always immoral. Some theologians, however, believe in the morality of stockpiling nuclear weapons as a deterrent against an enemy. To me, the Church has the right — and the obligation — to speak its views on the topic of war, and it should always be in defense of life at every stage.

---

[49] Ibid.

These issues — abortion, birth control, war, and so on — are so very difficult and complicated. But this is why we have been given the tremendous gift of our minds, so that we can reason things through and decide for ourselves what we believe is right and just. Your one obligation is to use your common sense and to follow your conscience, because that is always the bottom line: The conscience is supreme. Remember that Cardinal Joseph Ratzinger (Pope Benedict XVI) speaks of the ultimate tribunal as "one's own conscience," which has a place over every authority and "must be obeyed before all else, even, if necessary, against the requirement of ecclesiastical authority." He says the way conscience is formed cannot be left out of the question and, in the last resort, conscience is "transcendent ... beyond the claim of external social groups, even of the official Church."[50] Those are powerful words, and we should always keep them in mind, especially when dealing with such complicated, important issues like abortion and war.

---

[50] Cardinal Joseph Ratzinger (Pope Benedict XVI) (Commentary on the Documents of Vatican ll, ed. Vorgrimier,1968; on *Gaudium et Spes*, Part 1, Chapter 1).

"And so I tell you, Peter: you are a rock, and on this rock foundation I will build my church, and not even death will ever be able to overcome it. I will give you the keys of the Kingdom of heaven; what you prohibit on earth will be prohibited in heaven, and what you permit on earth will be permitted in heaven,"[51] Matthew 16:18–19.

Figure 11. Graphic layout by Brian Lee Sackett.

Chapter 8
I Believe! (... Or Do I?)

To be a good Catholic, what do you have to believe? The answer will probably surprise you. There are only about 30 things that are required. Some of them we've already discussed in previous chapters. For example, you need to believe in the real physical presence of Jesus in the Eucharist. In Holy Communion, the bread and wine actually become the physical body and blood of Jesus. He doesn't make the bread and wine look or taste like flesh and blood because that would be gross, but Catholics believe the Eucharist is His actual body and blood, soul and divinity, so that we might become blood brothers and sisters with Him and with each other. We've also discussed belief in the other sacraments by Jesus: baptism, reconciliation (confession), confirmation, holy orders, matrimony, and the sacrament of the sick.

Good Catholics must also believe in the things that are mentioned in the Nicene Creed. Formulated in 325 A.D., the Nicene Creed does not simply describe the reality of God; it defines that reality. Specifically, it defines who the Son is (and that the Son is in Himself, or God) and the relation between the Son and the one God, the Father; and God, the Holy Spirit. Each Sunday at Mass, we say the Nicene Creed:

We believe in one God, the Father, the Almighty, maker of heaven and earth. Of all that is seen and unseen. We believe in one Lord, Jesus Christ, the only Son of God, eternally begotten of the Father, God from God. Light from Light. True God from true God, begotten, not made, one in Being with the Father. Through him all things were made. For us men and for our salvation he came down from heaven; by the power of the

Holy Spirit he was born of the Virgin Mary and became man. For our sake he was crucified under Pontius Pilate; he suffered, died, and was buried. On the third day he rose again in fulfillment of the Scriptures; he ascended into heaven and is seated at the right hand of the Father. He will come again in glory to judge the living and the dead, and his kingdom will have no end. We believe in the Holy Spirit, the Lord, and giver of life, who proceeds from the Father and the Son. With the Father and the Son he is worshiped and glorified. He has spoken through the Prophets. We believe in one holy Catholic and apostolic Church. We acknowledge one baptism for the forgiveness of sins. We look for the resurrection of the dead, and the life of the world to come. Amen.

To be a good Catholic, you should also believe in the infallibility of the Pope. But what exactly does that mean? According to the dictionary, "infallibility" literally means "immunity from error." This is an extraordinary gift from the Holy Spirit by which the Catholic Church is protected from fundamental error in matters of faith and morals. It can be exercised by the Pope and by an ecumenical council. But infallibility does not lie within the person of the Pope. Instead, it lies within his office, as the head of the Church, and it does not pertain to every action of that office. When a Pope exercises that power, he has to clearly state that he is doing so. He has to declare, "This is an infallible statement." He does so by stating, *"ex cathedra."*

It is important to note that many Catholic theologians have taken a minimalist position, finding that only two papal pronouncements in history could be qualified as infallible. Those two pronouncements, which every good Catholic must believe, are the Immaculate Conception (1854) and the Assumption of Mary into heaven (1950). The dogma of the Immaculate Conception states that Mary, the mother of Jesus, was free from all sin (including the original sin) from the moment of her conception and throughout her entire life, even though she was completely human. This privilege was

bestowed upon her because she was the mother of the body of Jesus, the God-man.

The dogma of the Assumption of Mary into heaven states that when Mary died, she was taken up into heaven with her physical body. She did not do this on her own accord, like Jesus did when He rose from the dead and ascended into heaven under His own power. Instead she was given that privilege because she was the mother of the body of Jesus, who is God. Mary was not a goddess, but a complete human being.

So let me repeat myself: According to many theologians, only twice in history has the office of the Pope exercised its power of infallibility. Thus, when you read an article in the newspaper or on the Internet about the Pope expressing his comments on war, divorce, gay marriage, homosexuality, and so on, that is exactly what they are — his "comments." Thus, you have every right to question those comments, either agree or disagree, and then follow your conscience. And when you have followed your conscience, there should be no reason for you to so readily excommunicate yourself from the church.

Remember when Senator John Kerry was running for president and was denounced by certain priests and bishops for his positions on abortion and gay rights? Senator Kerry could have easily decided not to go to Holy Communion, but I am certain he exercised his Catholic right by thinking, praying, and then coming to his own conclusions that his conscience was true to himself.

Unfortunately, countless people, including many Catholics, have huge misconceptions about *"ex cathedra."* They mistakenly think that everything stated by the Pope (or the Church) is infallible. But let me quote the imminent theologian Fr. Richard McBrien. In his book, *Catholicism* (page 973), he states, "The Church has never explicitly claimed to speak infallibly on a moral question, so there is probably no instance as yet of a conflict between an individual's fallible decision in conscience and a teaching of the Church which is immune

from error."[52]

Part of the problem is that the media — and even some priests, for that matter — often perpetuate the misconception that the Pope or Church is always right. Sometimes we priests forget about educating our congregation about the true teachings of the Catholic Church. But we must continually teach the faith properly, logically, and clearly. Only then, I believe, will more people come to understand our gift of faith and share in that precious gift for the good of this life and the next. So it's no wonder why some Catholics think that they need to believe everything a priest, nun, deacon, bishop, or the Pope says. They think these Church authorities have an inside line directly to God, but that's just not the case.

The truth is that the clergy are merely human beings, just like everybody else, with their own strengths and weaknesses. Historically, there have been good popes and bad popes, good priests and bad priests, and so on. In chapter 5, I talked about how Jesus picked such a motley crew when He chose His 12 apostles. Thomas, the apostle, wouldn't believe in the resurrection until he touched Jesus physically. Judas sold Jesus for 30 pieces of silver, and the other apostles ran away when Jesus got into trouble with the law. What a disaster!

And consider whom Jesus picked to be the first Pope: Peter. In Matt 16:18–19, Jesus says to Peter, "And so I tell you, Peter: you are a rock, and on this rock foundation I will build my church, and not even death will ever be able to overcome it. I will give you the keys of the Kingdom of heaven; what you prohibit on earth will be prohibited in heaven, and what you permit on earth will be permitted in heaven."[53]

It appears that Jesus was going to give Peter something special when Jesus said to Peter, "I will give you the keys."

---

[52] Richard P. McBrien. *Catholicism.* New York:HarperCollins Publishers. 1994. p. 973.

[53] Scripture taken from the Good News Translation Catholic Edition – Second Edition, Copyright © 1992, by American Bible Society. Used by permission.

The word "keys" meant that Jesus was giving Peter the knowledge and understanding to explain the major things that were needed to unlock the gates of heaven, hence, the symbol of keys to open the gate, or way to heaven.

In John 21:17, Jesus conferred this when he commanded Peter to, "Take care of my sheep."[54] Jesus gave this command to Peter three times (which was considered "a sign" at that time). Jesus was giving Peter the authority to lead the Church. But Peter, the first Pope, was also the one who denied three times that he ever knew Jesus.

The point is that if the 12 apostles can make mistakes, then so can everyone else, including popes, bishops, priests, and other members of the clergy. Thus, you should always remember this: Although you need to take into account what the Catholic Church says, you can still question something unless it's dogma; that is, a statement concerning faith and morals that has been formally proclaimed by the Catholic Church. (Of course, if you consistently disregard everything that the Church says just because "the Church" says it, then I believe you are just being belligerent and perhaps the gift of faith in Catholicism is just not for you, and that's fine, too.)

The confusion about infallibility has often been made worse by the media. Here, the Catholic Church could do a much better job in its public relations. The problem is that many newspapers and other news media have no desire to make the Catholic Church look good. So they sometimes distort what the Pope says, or they take it out of context. Just remember this: If the Pope does make an infallible statement, all the local bishops and the parishes will surely let you know. And when the Pope is making an infallible statement, he needs to state, "This is an infallible statement," or *"ex cathedra."* To further clarify that, let me again quote Fr. Richard P. McBrien. In his book, *Catholicism* (page 764), he states:

1. "Vatican I defined certain conditions for the exercise of

---

54 Ibid.

the infallibility with which the pope is empowered. He is empowered with infallibility only when he is in the act of defining a doctrine of faith or morals, speaking as the head of the Church (*ex cathedra* "from the chair"), with the clear intention of binding the whole Church."

2.   "Infallibility is not a personal prerogative of the pope. He is empowered with the charism of infallibility only when he is in the act of defining a dogma of faith. It can be said, without exaggeration, that a pope who never defined a dogma of faith was never infallible. That would apply to such recent popes as John XXIII, Paul VI, John Paul I, and John Paul II."[55]

In other words, if something isn't spelled it out as dogma, then you can form your own opinion. Too many bishops and priests think they can speak *"ex cathedra,"* but don't buy it! If something sounds goofy or unreasonable, it probably is. Be an informed, thinking Catholic and don't leave the Church because you hear something that seems unreasonable. Rather, you should question the Church, because it is your God-given right.

---

[55] Ibid. p.764.

"Thank you, Jesus!"

Figure 12. Cartoonist Cliff Wirth.

Chapter 9

Gambling, Alcohol, Drugs, and Swearing

In the previous chapter, we talked about the various things all good Catholics need to believe. They must for example, believe in the dogma of the Immaculate Conception, which states that Mary, the mother of Jesus, was free from all sin (including the original sin) from the moment of her conception and throughout her entire life, even though she was completely human. In this chapter, I want to talk about other things that, to some people, might appear to go against Catholic teachings and beliefs. Specifically, do good Catholics gamble? Do they drink alcohol or take drugs? And do they swear?

Gambling

When I was a young boy, the major gambling scheme was called "the numbers racket," which was based on the horse races. People would add up the total of all the races and come up with three winning numbers. I never knew exactly how it worked, but my dad was an expert, not at winning, but at how the three numbers were obtained. I remember one Christmas Eve in 1936 when our family had only a nickel to our name. My dad played the number 406 because that was the post office box of my grandmother in Hubbell, Michigan.

Well, of all things, the winning number of the day turned out to be 406! My father won $25, which seemed like a million dollars at that time, because a loaf of bread was 8 cents and a gallon of gas was only a dime. I knew that this was a Christmas miracle and one of the best Christmases ever. And from that day on, I wanted to be either a numbers runner (the person who collects the money people have bet) or a priest. Fortunately (or maybe unfortunately?), I chose the less lucrative path.

From this early experience, I was hooked, always thinking I would win the megabucks and save the world from poverty. But today, I'm not much of a gambler, probably because of what happened with my father, who often gambled or drank away his monthly paycheck. Looking back, I think my father might have been addicted to gambling. He would always tell me, "What's in the blood can't be kicked out of the ass."

What does the Catholic Church say about gambling? When I was a child, I actually thought that the eighth sacrament was bingo because people would announce it at Mass every week. The Church's official stance is that everything is all right in moderation. If you can afford it and it isn't hurting anybody, then it's fine. But if it becomes compulsive, then it's wrong.

Some people will claim that gambling is wrong under any circumstances, no ifs, ands, or buts! Phooey. That kind of thinking only tells me that those people don't know their Scripture. In the Acts of the Apostles when Judas hung himself (1: 21–26), the other apostles had to replace him. So, they nominated two men who had been around Jesus: Justus and Matthias. And the apostles prayed that God would let them know which of the two men should replace Judas. Then they cast lots — kind of like drawing straws or rolling dice — and Matthias won to become the next apostle. (Justus would later become one of the original 72 disciples.) So you see, gambling was, and is still, a part of our Christian tradition!

Alcohol

My dad lived his life with gusto. Not only did he gamble, he also smoked five packs of cigarettes a day, drank like a fish, and died at 57 years of age. But did any good come out of his experiences? Well, as his son, I don't smoke or drink. So I guess that I learned by negative example and am healthier for it, although I suppose that some would say I'm a disgrace to my Irish ancestors. That reminds me of a joke: What's the difference between an Irish wake and an Irish wedding? One less drunk! All kidding aside, I believe that drinking, like gambling, is fine if done in moderation; that is, as long as you control the substance and it doesn't control you.

Many Catholics might be surprised to know that alcohol played such a prominent role in Jesus' first miracle. This happened at the wedding feast of Cana when Mary, Jesus' mother, noticed that the party was running out of wine. She didn't want to embarrass the bride and groom, so she asked her son for help. Jesus then changed six large jugs of water into wine. Voila, the first six-pack! Skeptics might claim that the liquid wasn't really alcohol, but according to Scripture, the stewards thought that it was the best they had every tasted.

Some people will call individuals with a drinking problem "drunks," while others refer to them as "alcoholics." The difference between the two is that alcoholics have to attend meetings. Sorry, I shouldn't be a smart-ass because it's not a laughing matter, and I should know because my dad was an alcoholic. (I guess maybe I tell jokes about the subject to ease the pain of some of my childhood memories.)

According to many medical experts, alcoholism is a disease, and once alcoholics have their first drink, they can't refrain from having the next, and the next, and the next. But alcoholism isn't a sin because people are born like that as a result of their genetic makeup. That is, they don't choose to be that way. Nevertheless, people with a hereditary inclination toward alcoholism must do everything possible to control the disease. For many, that means complete abstinence, which is far more easily said than done.

I remember my dad going to a clinic for "the cure," and on the way home, he stopped at a bar and celebrated for two months. What a tragedy for my mom and the rest of my family, to say nothing of how my father suffered.

When I was growing up, the Catholic Church had a program called, "The Pledge," in which people with a drinking problem promised that they would never have alcohol again. One of my uncles wanted to take the pledge and I went with him to see a priest. Unfortunately, this was the 10th time that my uncle was taking the pledge. The priest asked my uncle, "And how long to do you want to take 'The Pledge' for?"

And my uncle replied, "Father, I always take it for life." Sadly, I think that my uncle was actually drunk at the time.

Drugs

When I was an army chaplain in Vietnam with the 173th airborne, I met many, many American soldiers who were using illegal drugs. I always felt so horribly for those young men, who had such promising lives with so much to look forward to after the war. These GIs would tell me, "But Father, I can't stand this situation that I'm in. 'Nam is driving me crazy!"

And I would respond, "Yeah, but if you're taking drugs and aren't in control of your mind and body, then you are in no shape to be in combat, and you are risking not only your own life, but the lives of the people around you!"

I am not saying that drugs are inherently sinful because I realize how strong our instincts for relief can be. When I finish eating a dozen Krispy Kreme donuts in one sitting, I know how bad that is for my health. But that doesn't stop me, and I keep shoveling them in. I want the instant pleasure. But sometimes the need for relief or escape can get out of control, leading to only more misery.

I remember one young soldier in Vietnam who took a syringe and shot up with a liquid that he had been told was a new, more powerful drug. But the substance was dog piss and he lost his arm. I know what you're thinking. How stupid could he be? But what he did only shows how desperate he was for some kind of "high" to escape from the horrible daily realities of war. I also saw others coming into the medical tents with their noses bleeding. They had snorted what they thought was cocaine, only to discover that the powder was Comet, a kitchen cleanser.

Unfortunately, illegal drugs are not only a huge problem in war time. They have become a chronic problem that has reached every corner of the earth, destroying countless lives. To stop this scourge, you have to start with your own behavior. You, alone, can decide how you pick yourself up when you're down, whether it's through watching a TV show that makes you laugh, turning to your family and friends for comfort, eating a dozen donuts, or shooting yourself up with a highly addictive drug like heroin.

And we always need to remember that we do not live in the world by ourselves. We belong to, and are loved by, so many people, especially our families and our friends. Whatever we do affects not only ourselves, but also everyone we come in contact with. Please always remember that. And that's why I keep reminding you that you are the most important person in the world. God put you in this time and place to share your uniqueness. Don't mess that up, especially not by using drugs. And I tell you that not just for your own sake, but for that of those around you.

Swearing

Son of a bitch! Now that I have your attention, would you say that I just swore? Well, I don't think I was. To me, swearing is calling upon God to witness something, for example, by declaring, "I swear to God." Okay, then, is "son of a bitch" cursing? No, because cursing is defined as calling down some evil on another person or thing. Not to be nitpicky, but "son of a bitch" is really a profanity. The word "profanity" comes from the Latin pro, which means "before" or "outside," and fanum, which means "the temple." Thus, a profanity refers to language used "outside of church." So technically (and literally), if I use the same language "in" church, then it's not profanity, right? Maybe I think a little too much about words sometimes.

A while ago at our parish school, a first-grade girl came

111

running up to me, pointed at another girl, and said, "Father, she said a bad word."

So I asked, "What did she say?"

The little girl then told me, "She said 'shit.'"

I laughed and told her, "There are no bad words, but squealing is bad."

The disappointed little tattletale then said, "Oh, shit!"

For me, there might be words of bad taste, or words for emphasis, or slang words, but no words are in and by themselves bad. It's what you mean by those words.

Growing up in my family, we could say any words as long as they didn't have to do with sex, like the "f" word. In the army, though, I sure heard that word a lot. In fact, I almost wanted to buy stock in F*cking Inc. because that company seemed to manufacture just about everything we used: the f*cking rifles, the f*cking weapons, the f*cking tanks, the f*cking chow, and even the f*cking sergeant! Actually, I've been amazed at how, in the same sentence, the "f" word can be a noun, a pronoun, a verb, and an adjective. It has such a variety of meanings, depending on what inflection is used.

My mother was a real classy lady, but in her later years, her favorite expression was, "I'm pissed off." I also remember that when she got mad at me she would say, "You son of a bitch," and I would always reply, "Remember, Mom, I'm the 'son,' so you know what that makes you." That always made us both laugh, and sometimes she'd forget that she was mad at me in the first place.

Every subject in this chapter could be expounded *ad finitum*, or "to the end of time." In fact, people have written books on the subject of drug addiction alone, or on the topic of gambling or alcohol abuse. But we all basically know what is right and what is wrong, what is truly important and what is not. This is why God gave us a conscience, and that conscience is supreme. After all, words are just words. It's what you mean behind those words that really count.

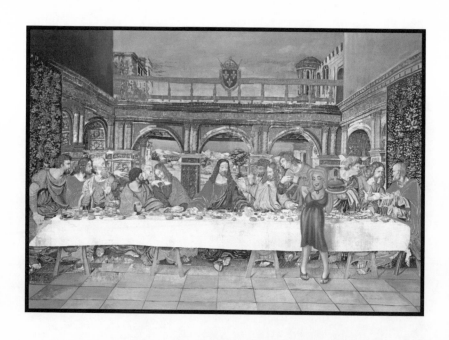

Figure 13. Picture furnished by Hamburger Mary's in
Las Vegas, Nevada. With permission.

Chapter 10
Exploring Different Religious Ideas

Religion has long been an important part of humanity and a major inspiration in literature, music, painting, sculpture, architecture, education, and life in general. Five religions have had a major effect on civilization: Christianity, Islam, Hinduism, Buddhism, and Judaism. Together, their current combined membership is nearly 4 billion people, or about 80 percent of the world's total population. Other religions are just as important to their followers, but those five seem to have had the greatest impact on the world in general.

Obviously, each religion could be explored *ad infinitum*, and in fact, countless books have been written to help you learn more. But that's not my goal here. Instead, the purpose of this chapter is to help you appreciate just a small sampling of the various religious ideas around the world. Each of them might promise the ultimate truth, but they can't all be true, especially when many hold views that are contrary to each other, because God never contradicts Himself. Nevertheless, each religious idea may contain goodness and partial truth.

In addition to the major religions, I will also discuss several smaller sects like Mormonism that are among the fastest growing in the world. My purpose is not to put those groups down, but to ask some important questions of them. To me, it's never wrong to question anything. But if you ask a question, then you must do so with a sincere heart if you are really seeking the truth. And you have to listen to the answer and make an honest attempt to understand it, although you don't necessarily have to accept that answer.

That said, let's explore some different religious ideas with an openness to think logically, to disseminate, and to draw our own conclusions. Again, my purpose is not to give a full description of complicated concepts. For that, you should consult each religion directly to learn more. Instead, my goal here is just to explore some religions to understand how they might be similar to, as well as different from, Catholicism.

Born-again Christianity

Most born-again religions think that you have to accept their beliefs to be part of their group and get into heaven. They often quote John 3:5: "I am telling you the truth," replied Jesus, "that no one can enter the Kingdom of God unless he is born of water and the Spirit."[56] To born-again Christians, this means that you have to "accept Jesus as your personal savior." Of the numerous religious groups that claim their beliefs are essential for salvation, two of the most popular are Hope Chapel and Calvary Chapel.

Hope Chapel is a member of the Four Square Gospel Church, founded in 1923 by Aimee Semple McPherson of Los Angeles. McPherson based her movement on the understanding of the four roles of Jesus Christ: savior, baptizer, healer, and coming king. Her doctrine includes fundamentalist and Pentecostal emphasis: sanctification, baptism of the Holy Spirit, the gift of tongues, Christ as savior and healer, and the imminent return of Christ. Services consist of entertaining musical groups, preaching, testimonies, and healings.

Much of McPherson's success has been attributed to her personality, but scandal repeatedly touched her personal life, most notably in 1926, when she disappeared for a month, then surfaced with a story that she had been kidnapped. Later, people learned that she had been on a romantic tryst. In 1944, McPherson died from an accidental overdose of barbiturates, and the church leadership was passed on to her son, Rolf McPherson. Today, there are hundreds of congregations of Hope Chapels, with thousands of members.

---

[56] Ibid.

The other successful born-again group is called Calvary Chapel, which came out of the Jesus movement in 1960 through the 1970s. Calvary Chapel views God in a miraculous way. In their expression of faith, members do not rely on reason but instead, on emotion, and the important thing for them is their personal relationship with God. Services are informal, flexible, and open, as they are guided by the Holy Spirit.

During a service, contemporary music is played and a message is sent by someone with a guitar (who, to me, looks like a hippie), as opposed to a robed choir and a pipe organ. Bible teachings are the basis for the sermons, and members believe that Christ's promise of salvation, redemption, and forgiveness is for everyone, regardless of how they look or how they choose to worship, just as long as they accept Jesus as their "personal savior."

That view runs contrary to the Catholic belief that faith in Jesus Christ is a gift, as noted in Scripture (John 6:44) when Jesus says, "Stop grumbling among yourselves. No one can come to me unless the Father who sent me draws him to me; and I will raise him to life on the last day."[57] Thus, Catholics believe that faith is a free gift that no one can bring upon themselves unless God wills it. On the other hand, no one can be condemned if they did not receive it. So Catholics believe that everyone can have eternal salvation because of Jesus.

Moreover, even before Vatican II, the Catholic Church said there were three types of baptism: (1) baptism of water, which is the most common form, (2) baptism of blood, which applies to those who gave their physical lives for Jesus, including the martyrs who were killed because they would not renounce their belief in Jesus, and (3) baptism of desire, which means that as long as a person has followed his conscience to the best of his ability, he will be "saved" by Jesus.

---

[57] Ibid.

Church of Jesus Christ of Latter-day Saints

You cannot find more clean-living and dedicated people than the Mormons. They, along with the Coca-Cola Company, are tireless in their efforts to reach people around the world. A friend of mine who's a priest has traveled to some of the most remote areas of South America. He once told me that whenever they arrived at a location where no missionary had ever been, they were always greeted by a Coca-Cola sign. We could probably all learn from the Coke people how to do a better job of spreading the gospel.

Mormonism was founded in 1830 in New York by the prophet, Joseph Smith. He believed that the fundamental principles of his religion were the testimony of the apostles and prophets concerning Jesus Christ. Mormons believe that Jesus died, was buried, and rose to ascend into heaven. But contrary to what Mormons say, they are not recognized as a Christian religion by the other Christian denominations. This is because Mormons do not recognize the Holy Trinity. In the teachings of their prophet, Joseph Smith, he states, "God himself was once as we are now, and is an exalted man, and sits enthroned in yonder heavens! That is the great secret."[58] This seems to say that God was once a human being, and it also appears to imply that we humans could possibly become divine. (For a clearer explanation, you should consult with the official Church of Jesus Christ of Latter-day Saints for more details.)

In reality, the story of Mormonism reads like a mystery novel, with secret visions, golden tablets, magic eyeglasses, and numerous other subplots. Basically, the Mormons believe that the original Church that Jesus established in 33 A.D. went into apostasy (meaning that the original teachings of Jesus were distorted) and had to be restored 1,500 years later by their prophet Smith. But if that were true, then Jesus must have lied in Scripture (Matthew 16:18) when He attests to the following:

---

[58] Smith, J.F. *Teaching of the Prophet Joseph Smith.* Salt Lake City, Utah: Deseret Book Company. 1976.

"And so I tell you, Peter: you are a rock, and on this rock foundation I will build my church, and not even death will ever be able to overcome it."[59] Here, Jesus Christ also affirms that nothing — no person or thing — will be able to destroy His Church. Thus, there couldn't have been a total apostasy. In Matthew 28:18–20, again, Jesus says, "I have been given all the authority in heaven and on earth. Go, then, to all peoples everywhere and make them my disciples: baptize them in the name of the Father, the Son, and of the Holy Spirit, and teach them to obey everything I have commanded you. And I will be with you always, to the end of the age."[60]

Another big difference between Mormons and Catholics is that Mormons believe that only they can reach the highest state of heaven. Called the "Celestial Kingdom," that state is God's personal community — a place where Mormon families believe they can be together for all eternity. They can achieve that by: (1) faith in Jesus Christ, (2) repentance, (3) baptism by immersion for the remission of sins (by someone who holds the appropriate priesthood authorization by the Latter-day Saints Church), and (4) laying on of hands for the gift of the Holy Spirit.

Mormons also believe that there are two lesser levels of heaven, depending on how you have lived your life. The "Terrestrial Kingdom" is the everlasting place of residence for those who have accepted their teachings of Christ during their life on earth, but did not live up to those beliefs. These people know the greatness of God, but will not live as a family unit in heaven. They will have the privilege of Jesus in their midst, but only occasionally. And the lowest degree of heaven is called the "Telestial World," which is for those who did not follow the teachings of Jesus (as believed by the Mormons). But before these individuals can arrive at the Telestial World, they

---

59 Scripture taken from the Good News Translation Catholic Edition – Second Edition, Copyright © 1992, by American Bible Society. Used by permission.
60 Ibid.

must first suffer in hell, paying for their actions on earth. (Obviously, for a more thorough explanation of the three states of heaven, you need to contact the Mormon Church.)

In contrast, Catholics believe that everyone, including people of other religions as well as those without a religion, will go to heaven and be in the presence of God as long as they have followed their conscience to the best of their ability. Catholics believe this because Jesus died for us all, each and every one of us.

The Jehovah's Witnesses

Who holds the Guinness world record for having had the most doors slammed at them? I am sure you already know the answer. The Jehovah's Witnesses are the most zealous missionaries of all. If I had a penny for every time someone told them, "Get off my porch!" I think I would be rich. The Jehovah's Witnesses are familiar figures at the front doors of people all over the world. They are always polite, but very persistent.

The Jehovah's Witnesses were founded in Pennsylvania in the 1870s by Charles Taze Russell. Although they consider themselves Christians, they, like the Mormons, do not believe in the Holy Trinity or in the divinity of Jesus. They have their own translation of the Bible, from which they quote freely. They state that their Bible is from the "original languages," but not the "original manuscripts" (because none are in existence). Their translation of John 1:1 reads, "In (the) beginning the Word was, and the Word was with God, and the Word was (a) god." Does this imply that there are several gods?

Church members who have knocked on my door have explained to me how their founder, President Russell, taught that to redeem is to buy back. When I've asked them what Christ bought back for all men, they tell me that President Russell's answer to that question was the word "life." Man lost this life by the disobedience of the "first Adam," and the "second Adam" (Christ) bought it back with his own life.

I find it interesting that the Jehovah's Witnesses believe that only 144,000 of them will get to heaven. The rest will be the obedient subjects of the Lord in paradise on earth. Whenever I am invited to join their religion, I always ask them, "How many members does your church currently have?" and they answer, "Over six and a half million!" Then I ask, "If only 144,000 can get to heaven, then what is the point of my joining, or why, then, should you be making such efforts to recruit?" I've never gotten what I would consider to be a good answer to that question.

The Da Vinci Code

Every so often, a new religious idea comes about and creates quite a stir. A recent example is the controversy surrounding *The Da Vinci Code*, the best-selling novel written by Dan Brown. The book, which has been adapted into a film starring Tom Hanks, describes a secret society that was supposed to have existed during the time of Leonardo da Vinci. According to the book, the group knew certain secrets that, if revealed, would shake the very foundations of Christianity. (The implication is that the Vatican has been trying to keep this information under wraps for centuries.) The great painter da Vinci was supposedly a member of this secret society and, so the story goes, he revealed the earth-shattering secrets in his paintings.

Perhaps the most shocking revelation is that Jesus, the Son of God, was not divine, but a man that was deified by the Vatican at the Council of Nicea. *The Da Vinci Code* says that Jesus was also married to Mary Magdalene and that He fathered children with her. That secret was supposedly revealed by da Vinci in his famous painting, "The Last Supper." The novelist, Brown, explains that, in the painting, there appears to be a woman to Jesus' right. (Remember that, as the Bible states, only the apostles were seated with Jesus at the Last Supper.) According to Brown, that woman is Mary Magdalene.

Brown also goes on to explain that throughout history, people have searched for the "Holy Grail" — the cup or vessel that Jesus used at the Last Supper when He instituted Holy Communion, saying, "This is the vessel of my blood." Leonardo da Vinci did, indeed, paint a cup in front of Jesus, as well as for all the apostles, for a total of 13 cups. The cups were tiny, stemless, and made of glass, but the painting doesn't contain a chalice, or large cup, that might have been the Holy Grail.

This leads the author, Brown, to claim that Mary Magdalene was the vessel, or Holy Grail, and the mother of Jesus' children. Brown also describes other supposedly hidden clues and symbols in da Vinci's painting to justify the claim that Jesus and Mary Magdalene were actually married.

The main problem here is that many people don't seem to realize that *The Da Vinci Code* is a novel. That is, it's a work of fiction. Some people actually think the book's contents are historical fact and not the creative product of a novelist's imagination. I have my own theory of the painting. The person to Jesus' right is John the apostle, Jesus' beloved disciple. Actually, John the apostle was a cross-dresser, which is why he appears in the painting to be so feminine.

Now, for those of you who believe my theory, I'd like to sell you a bridge in Brooklyn. Others of you might rightfully think my theory is pure hogwash, but I don't believe it's any more ridiculous than the *The Da Vinci Code* assertion that Jesus was married to Mary Magdalene.

It's important to remember that the da Vinci painting is not a Kodak photograph. That is, Leonardo da Vinci wasn't present at the Last Supper to paint Jesus and the apostles. And, in fact, the painting is hardly historically accurate. During the time of the Last Supper, people did not eat at a big dining-room table. Instead, they would lie on pillows on the floor, and the table would be very low to the ground, something like a Japanese *chabudai*. Also, if Mary Magdalene had been sitting at the table next to Jesus, then there would have been only 11 apostles present (and we can recognize Judas in Leonardo da

Vinci's painting, with the money bag). So where was John, Jesus' best friend? Why wouldn't he have been present? So, although *The Da Vinci Code* might be a fun novel to read, filled with its fair share of suspense and thrills, it should hardly be taken as gospel.

Judaism

Judaism, which dates back nearly 4,000 years, is the parent religion of Christianity and Islam. Abraham was not its founder, but a key figure as the first Hebrew to receive a revelation from God. Judaism is more than a system of beliefs; it gives a sense of identity and tradition that binds together families and all fellow Jews. The more that Christians and Moslems know about Judaism, the more they can understand their own faith. For instance, the Old Testament of the Bible deals with God's revelation to the Jewish community, their laws, and the prophesies of the Messiah coming into the world.

Ironically, even though Jesus and all the apostles were Jewish, Christians (and Moslems) have persecuted Jews throughout history. Some Christians still blame Jews for the death of Jesus Christ. But how can the Jewish people of today be responsible for anything that occurred so long ago? Should all of us, then, be held responsible for any atrocities committed by our ancestors?

After centuries of such oppression, Pope John Paul II issued a public apology on behalf of the Catholic Church and asked for forgiveness. As an indication of his sincerity, Pope John Paul II mentioned just two living people in his will: his longtime secretary and Elio Toaff, "the rabbi of Rome."

Islam

Although many Christians and Jews do not want to hear this, they actually have more in common with Moslems than they do with people of other religious faiths, because they all worship one true God. Islam might refer to God by the name

"Allah" (an Arabic term comprising two words: *Al*, which means "the," and *illah*, which means "God"), but Moslems are similar to Christians and Jews in that all three major religions are monotheistic; that is, they believe that there is but one God.

Moslems, however, differ in their belief that God's prophet is Mohammed. And the main difference between Christianity and the other two religions (Islam and Judaism) is that we believe that Jesus is divine, as He claimed, whereas Moslems believe that Mohammed was mortal and Jews believe that Moses was mortal. Interestingly, the Islamic Holy Book, or Koran, contains not only their Holy Scripture, but also the Gospel of Jesus as well as the Jewish Torah.

You can learn so much from Judaism, Christianity, and Islam, but it would take volumes to do any of them justice. So, if you want more information, you have to do further research. Unfortunately, because of the past cruelty and violence inflicted by these religions in many countries and lands (some of which continues to take place today), there is great distrust between the three major faiths. Sadly, all this runs so contrary to the tolerance that was taught by Christ, Moses, and Mohammed.

Hinduism

Hinduism is among the world's oldest religions. Its followers believe in many gods, numbering in the thousands, but they recognize one supreme spirit called Brahman ("the absolute"). Hindus are in a continuous process of rebirth, or reincarnation. At death, their deeds (or karma) will determine what their next life will be. The goal is to break this cycle of birth, death, and rebirth, which is called "the wheel of life," so that they can gain release and merge with Brahman in a condition of spiritual perfection called *moksha*.

Buddhism

Jesus was the only major prophet in the history of the world who claimed to be God. Neither Moses nor Mohammed nor Buddha ever made such a claim. In fact, Buddha didn't even raise the issue of whether there was a God or not. In actuality, he thought the question was irrelevant.

Buddha taught enlightenment, which he defined as the simple, clear realization of the most basic truths about life. According to him, the four noble truths are that: (1) life is difficult, (2) all hardship and suffering come from inappropriate attachment or grasping, (3) to avoid suffering, people need to avoid inappropriate craving, and (4) to stop inappropriate craving, people must follow the eight-fold noble path, which requires wisdom, ethics, and concentration.

To me, Buddhism is more a philosophy of life than a religion, and the Buddhism that was taught by Buddha is very different from the Buddhism that is practiced in many places today. An example is Nichiren Soshu of America, an evangelical Buddhist sect that guarantees happiness through chanting, which is a simplistic form of Buddhism.

On a personal level, I find Buddhism's emphasis on life's hardships depressing, but I do admire the self-control and dedication of many Buddhists. I realize that my brief description is not doing Buddhism any justice, but if you're interested in learning more, I highly recommend that you read books on the subject.

The Church of Scientology

The Church of Scientology is another group that is called a religion, even though members are not required to believe in a personal God or gods. People can decide that for themselves, and the Church of Scientology offers no specific dogma on the subject. Founded in 1954 by the science-fiction writer L. Ron Hubbard of Los Angeles, the Church of Scientology began as a "self-awareness group" that helped people to achieve happiness. Hubbard never claimed it was divinely revealed or that he ever had a vision. However, because its members found it so spiritually satisfying, they (and not Hubbard) deemed it worthy of church status. Many people believe that Scientology doesn't believe in a Supreme Being, but in his book, *Science of Survival*, Hubbard wrote,

No culture in the history of the world, save the thoroughly depraved and expiring ones, has failed to affirm the existence of a Supreme Being. It is an empirical observation that men without a strong and lasting faith in a Supreme Being are less capable, less ethical and less valuable to themselves and society ... A man without an abiding faith is, by observation alone, more of a thing than a man.[61]

Perhaps the Church of Scientology is best known for its celebrity members, including Tom Cruise, the movie star. Interestingly, in his younger years, Cruise actually grew up Catholic, and he even was in the seminary for a year. (I am sorry that we, the Catholic Church, did not meet his spiritual needs.)

Membership in the Church of Scientology can be costly. Friends of mine who were involved in the movement have told me how expensive the required counseling sessions became because they had to continue buying all the required tapes and books, which are their scriptures according to L. Ron Hubbard.

There are a few things I would like to ask Scientologists. My own personal question to them is, "Did the Supreme Being create us and then abandon us?" I'd also like to know what happens to people after they die, according to Scientology.

For the most accurate answers, you should obviously ask the Church of Scientology directly to obtain its beliefs concerning this subject, but I'll try my best here to summarize its stance. Many Scientologists are certain that they have lived past lives and individual members are free to believe this or not. Past lives are not a dogma of the Church but members can believe for themselves that they have lived before, that they

61 *What Is Scienctology? The Comprehensive Reference on the World's Fastest Growing Religion.* Los Angeles, CA:Bridge Publications Inc. 1992.

had an identity prior to the current one.

Scientology gives people tools to handle upsets from their past lives in order to free them to live happier lives in the present. Here, Scientologists aren't really talking about reincarnation, which generally refers to being born in different life-forms. Scientologists believe that a person can be born again into the flesh or body of another individual. I'm not sure, though, whether that means you would lose your present identity and become someone else. If that's the case, I would surmise that you would never see your mother, father, siblings, children, other relatives, and friends again after you die.

For me, one of the beauties of our Christian faith is that we believe in the physical resurrection of the body and life everlasting after we enter heaven. In order to be a complete human being in heaven (and on earth), we need both a body and a soul. Only in heaven, though, does the union between the two become perfect in every way. We do not become angels in heaven; angels are spiritual beings, a different entity. We always remain human, but in heaven, we become beings. And because we remain human, we still have our relationships with our family and friends. Many Christians find that comforting. I know that I do. So, once we come into existence, we forever retain who we are. What a great gift this is from God, and Jesus proved it through His own resurrection by His own power.

Kabbalah

One of the latest religious fads is the revival of Jewish mysticism referred to by the name "Kabbalah." Many say it was handed down orally from Abraham. But despite this claim of antiquity, the movement appears to have been given its earliest formulation in the 11th century in France, spreading from there to Spain.

Kabbalistic interpretation of Scripture is based on the belief that every word, letter, number, and even accent, contains various mysteries that can be interpreted by those who know the "secret." For instance, the names of God are believed to contain miraculous power, and each letter of the divine name is considered potent. That's why Kabbalistic signs and writings are often used as amulets and in magical practices.

Much of the religion is explained in the book *The Power of Kabbalah*, by Yehuda Berg, which has been endorsed by Madonna, the pop singer and actress of "Material Girl" fame. Madonna believes there is no magic or hocus-pocus in the movement, and she contends that the book has nothing to do with religious dogmas but has ideas that are startling, yet easy to understand.

For example, the book talks about the Big Bang theory, which postulates that the universe originated billions of years ago from a single dense point of nearly infinite energy. (That theory, by the way, was first postulated by Fr. Georges Lemaitre, a Catholic priest, in 1927.) Madonna calls the idea of the Big Bang theory simple (well, she's a genius if she fully understands it).

Recently in the local Las Vegas paper, I've seen an ad inviting people to attend lectures on the "Free Power of Kabbalah," promoting "Free Kabbalistic Palm, Face, and Astrology Readings." So I question those claims that the Kabbalah movement doesn't involve hocus-pocus. But don't get me wrong. I don't mean to put Kabbalah down; I'm just saying that its mysticism may not be for everyone.

After reading this chapter, you're probably wondering why I've included it in a book about Catholicism. My purpose was to help you realize that the human race, from its very beginning, has long craved to know how we came into existence. Was there a Creator, and is He or She still interested in our welfare? And what happens to us when we die? Is there an afterlife, or do we just cease to exist?

We could reason from logic that there had to have been a first cause, which we might call "God," but exactly what is He or She like? Catholics believe that God revealed Himself many times throughout history and that He did so completely when He came to earth as Jesus, the God-man and second person of the Holy Trinity. Previous to that, people might have had a glimpse of God through nature and through His revealing Himself to certain peoples, such as the people of Israel. But not until Jesus came to earth did people receive the whole story. And the story is that God loves us so much that He became one of us by uniting His divinity to our humanity in Jesus. So now we know that God can understand completely what human beings go through in life. When you think of how Jesus sacrificed for us, you'll realize beyond a shadow of a doubt how much God loves us.

For me, one of the beauties of our Catholic faith is that you do not have to be a Roman Catholic to get to heaven. So we don't have an obligation to shove our views down someone else's throat to "save" that person (unlike other fanatic religions).

Nevertheless, we know that not all members of the Catholic Church have always followed this basic teaching of religious freedom and the right to follow one's conscience. The Inquisition and the Crusades are just two of the most egregious examples of religious fanaticism that can never be defended. The most charitable explanation is that Church authorities thought they were protecting people from becoming spiritually corrupt. But even that is no excuse for those past excesses.

In Catholicism, faith in Jesus Christ is a gift, as it states in Scripture (John 6:43–44) when Jesus says, "Stop grumbling among yourselves. People cannot come to me unless the Father who sent me draws them to me; and I will raise them to life on the last day."[62] In other words, faith is a free gift, and people can't bring it upon themselves unless God wills it. At the same time, people can't be condemned if they do not receive it. Therefore, we can all be saved, or have eternal salvation,

---

[62] Scripture taken from the Good News Translation Catholic Edition – Second Edition, Copyright © 1992, by American Bible Society. Used by permission.

because of Jesus, even if we aren't even aware of that. God gave us free will, which makes us human beings who are responsible for our actions. And, for some reason, He does not give the gift of faith in Jesus to everyone. But those whom He chooses are specially blessed.

So the next logical question is this: If God loves all people equally, why doesn't He give everyone the gift of faith? I really don't know the answer to that, but I do know that God always does what's best for a person, just like a loving parent. And I also know that different people have different needs. So, for whatever reason, some people might, at certain times in their lives, be better off without the gift of faith. But that doesn't change the bottom line that God loves everybody equally, every race, creed, and religion.

To me, true Catholicism really makes so much sense. Rigid Christianity, on the other hand, makes no sense at all, especially when it casts God as a bogeyman. Many born-again Christians are only too thrilled to let you know that they are "saved" and that you aren't. What self-righteous bastards! I know from my own life that my Catholic faith is the biggest blessing I could ever have received, and because of that, I want you to have that gift too, but only if you, yourself, desire it.

The second greatest blessing is my family and friends. Because of them, I truly feel that I am one of the most fortunate people in the world (although that doesn't mean that I haven't had any shit in my life!). All that is what makes me who and what I am, and I wouldn't change anything in my entire life. This, I know, may sound like bullshit to many people, but it really isn't. It's how I honestly feel, and I am forever grateful for that.

Figure 14 caption. Damien Drawing from a Journey from Cashmere to his Home in Hawaii, Edward Clifford, London: Macmillan and co.,1889.

"The political and journalistic world can boast of very few heroes who compare with Father Damien of Molokai ..."
~ *Mahatma Gandhi*

Chapter 11

Everything Else You Wanted to Know about Catholicism but Never Had a Chance to Ask (Part 1)

When I was a young boy in Catholic grade school, I was fascinated with stories about the saints. Each story was different (and some were even weird), but I knew that the saints were very close to God, and thus, it became my goal to become one of them. So I thought I would begin my "holy training" early by imitating some of the saints. I began by putting a pebble in my shoe, wearing a cord around my waist, and sleeping on the bare floor. Did all that make me holy? No, it only gave me a sore foot, a bruised belly, and a backache. But I thought I was on the right track.

Then I heard about St. Lawrence, the deacon who lived in 258 A.D. He, like many other saints, died horribly. Because he refused to worship the Roman gods, St. Lawrence was slowly roasted to death. Somehow, though, he managed to retain a sense of humor to the end. When he was halfway roasted, as the story goes, he said to his torturers, "Turn me over. I'm done on this side." I guess this proves that he was a true religious "friar." Sorry, that was a bad joke, but after hearing that story, this young boy thought he would take a different road to sainthood.

What Are Saints?

But just what is a saint? Simply put, a saint is someone who goes to heaven. Huh? Yes, as long as someone gets into heaven, then that is what that person is called — a saint.

135

Therefore, someday, we could all be saints, but maybe we won't be "canonized" saints. For a person to become a canonized saint, the Church has to officially declare that that individual is in heaven. (Of course, you can still be in heaven even though the Church doesn't officially declare it.)

Although Pope Alexander III began the process of canonization in the 12th century, the Church had recognized many people as saints prior to that, including Mary, the mother of God; St. Joseph, the foster father of Jesus; the apostles; and the prophets of the Old Testament. Today, canonization is more complicated, requiring the investigation of an individual's complete life, from birth to death, and the verification of at least two miracles attributed to the intercession of that person (that is, the person asking for and receiving help from God).

Many saints got to heaven before the Church instituted the process of canonization, and many more arrived there after that, even though they had not been officially canonized. One such person is Fr. Damien, a priest who lived in the 19th century. He, like Jesus Christ, gave his life for people here on earth. Not only did Fr. Damien devote himself to living with, helping, and serving all the men, women, and children stricken with leprosy in Kalaupapa, on the Hawaiian island of Molokai, he also literally gave his life to that cause — he died after contracting the disease. Because of his unselfish dedication, he inspired people to look for and ultimately discover a cure for leprosy, or Hansen's disease. And so the world has one more saint like Fr. Damien to emulate. I feel particularly close to him because, when I was young, I was inspired to become a priest after reading about his life.

Unfortunately, most of those saints who have been canonized are priests and nuns, not everyday people who might be just as deserving. That's because, to be canonized, a person would need an organization with the time and money to push his or her cause, and most families do not have those kinds of resources.

How Do Saints Get Their Names?

The Church names many saints for something they did. Take, for example, the story of how St. Christopher became known as the "Christ bearer." One day at a river that was flooded and very dangerous to cross, Christopher saw a boy who was desperate to get to the other side. So Christopher risked his life to carry the boy on his shoulders across the river. Well, as it turned out, the young boy was actually Jesus, and hence the name, "the Christ bearer." Christopher was a saint who also carried others across the river bed on his shoulders because that area had no bridge.

Another story concerns St. Veronica, a woman who met Jesus when He was carrying His cross before His crucifixion. She saw Him bleeding, so she ran to Him and wiped His face with a towel. When she removed the towel from Jesus' face, His image appeared on the cloth, hence her name Veronica, or *Vera Icona* (*vera* meaning "true" and *icona* meaning "image"). Whatever they are named, though, always remember that saints were just human beings who followed their conscience to the best of their ability.

How Can Mary Be the Mother of God?

One question people often ask is, "Isn't it a contradiction to say that God had a mother?" But what we really mean is that Mary is the mother of the body of Jesus (who is God). Mary is the first among saints, and she is so very special. When she was asked by the angel Gabriel to be the mother of the Messiah, she said, "You got to be kidding!"

But Gabriel said, "No, I'm serious."

So Mary asked, "How can that be? I have never been with a man."

The angel Gabriel then told her, "The Holy Spirit will overshadow you, and the child will be the son of the Most High."

And Mary said, "Be it done to me according to your will."

To appreciate why Mary is so very special, you have to understand that she was a good, devout Jewish woman who knew her prophecies. She realized that by agreeing to the angel Gabriel's request, she would have to endure tremendous pain and sorrow when the Messiah was put to death. Yet she still said yes. That's why, through all of history, people have had such reverence and respect for her.

Because Mary agreed to be the mother of Jesus, God gave her two special gifts: the Immaculate Conception (Mary was conceived without original sin) and the Assumption (after Mary died, she was physically taken into heaven). We say that she was assumed, or taken up fully, in both her body and soul (unlike Jesus, who rose from the dead under his own power and returned to heaven physically and spiritually).

Many people don't know that the very first miracle that Jesus performed was done at Mary's request. She wanted to save a wedding couple from embarrassment when they ran out of wine. So she asked her son for help, and Jesus changed some water into wine. Mary, herself, was not divine but a human being, and thus, she could not perform any miracles on her own. So she asked God for help, just as we do.

Contrary to what many born-again Christians tell us, Catholics don't pray *to* Mary. Instead we pray *with* her. That's why we say, "Hail Mary, full of grace, pray for us." (By the way, the word "grace" here means "God's life.") The beauties of Mary are many, but perhaps the greatest thing about her is that she was human, just like we are. Mary is not a goddess, and to make her one would do her an injustice. This confuses people who aren't Catholic because they mistakenly think we put her on par with Jesus. That misconception might be because of the numerous apparitions of Mary that people have claimed, including Our Lady of Lourdes, Our Lady of Fatima, and Our Lady of Medjugorje, to name just a few. The Catholic Church states that you can accept these or not as they are private revelations, but you must accept the revelations of Jesus, which ended with the death of the last apostle, John the Evangelist.

I remember talking to a missionary priest who had gone into a remote town in the Amazon, where he discovered a beautiful church built in honor of the Blessed Virgin Mary. The parish had not had a priest for years, so at the first Sunday he was there, he gave a sermon on the divinity of Jesus. After that Mass, people thanked him for his sermon and said they had never heard about Jesus before. How sad!

How Does One Attain Eternal Life?

Through the ages, people have long wondered how they might attain eternal life. In the Bible, that very question was asked of Jesus (Matthew 19:16–22):

Once a man came to Jesus. "Teacher," he asked, "what good must I do to receive eternal life?" "Why do you ask me concerning what is good?" answered Jesus. "There is only One who is good. Keep the commandments if you want to enter life [that is, go to heaven and be with God]." "What commandments?" he asked. Jesus answered, "Do not commit murder; do not commit adultery; do not steal; do not accuse anyone falsely; respect your father and your mother; and love your neighbor as you love yourself." "I have obeyed all these commandments," the young man replied. "What else do I need to do?" Jesus said to him, "If you want to be perfect, go and sell all you have and give the money to the poor, and you will have riches in heaven; then come and follow me." When the young man heard this, he went away sad, because he was very rich.[63]

When I was ordained to the priesthood in 1958, I received thousands of dollars as ordination gifts. Remembering the above Scripture, I gave all that money to the poor. Another

---

63 Scripture taken from the Good News Translation Catholic Edition – Second Edition, Copyright © 1992, by American Bible Society. Used by permission.

time, I even gave my car away. But did that act of charity make me holy? Hell, no, but it did make me chronically late: Nobody ever knew when I would show up for Mass because, without a car, I had to hitchhike. Talk about a bummer!

Remember that Jesus didn't say, "Blessed are the poor." Instead, He said, "Blessed are the poor in spirit." That means, don't be overly attached to things. In other words, don't let your material possessions own you. But you do need certain things to survive, like food and both a refrigerator to keep it from spoiling and a stove to cook it, a home with a heating system to keep you from freezing in the winter (unless you live in Hawaii), and so on.

To be poor sometime in your life might be a blessing, because then you can later relate to — and have compassion for — the needy. But to be poor your entire life would be a curse. And if you gave all your possessions to the poor, what would society have? One more poor person! To find happiness in this life, you not only need spiritual, physical, and mental stability, you also need financial stability. If any one of these necessities is missing, your life could be a miserable existence, and I am sure that Jesus would not want that.

Why Do We Pray?

According to Catholic tradition, prayer is the lifting of the mind and heart to God. We may also refer to prayer as talking to God, with our minds and our hearts. As Catholics, we believe that you can pray only to God, but you may pray along with the Virgin Mary, the saints, and others. The Nicene Creed, which was formulated in 325 A.D., talks about the "Communion of Saints," meaning "the faithful on earth, the faithful in heaven, and all the souls of purgatory." This makes up the body of Christ — the Church united with the Holy Trinity. Because we are one family (the Church family) and family members are close to each other, we can ask them individually or collectively to talk to God for or with us.

Other religions might think that we are praying to (or

worshipping) Mary and all the rest of the saints, but that is not so because those individuals don't have the power to answer our prayers. Rather, we Catholics are asking Mary and the other saints to help us by praying with us, to God the Almighty. They, like us, are only human beings. Yes, holy as they all are, saints do pray (that is, talk) to God. Sometimes it is through the intercession of a saint, who prays to God, that certain miracles occur. That's why we ask the saints to pray with us. Many people, including non-Catholic Christians, contend that Mary and the saints can't intervene on our behalf. But they can. Remember that Jesus' first miracle was performed because Mary asked Him for help at the wedding feast of Cana.

Please remember that there are many ways to pray. There are formal prayers, like The Lord's Prayer, The Hail Mary, and The Rosary. There is also spontaneous prayer — talking to God, making it up as you go along. Then there are liturgical prayers: The holy Mass and the holy sacraments (which are very important forms of community worship for Catholics). If you are wondering about the "perfect prayer," it is the holy sacrifice of the Mass, when we receive Holy Communion. As I explained in chapter 5, this is when we become blood brothers and sisters with Jesus and with each other. It's what Jesus commanded us to do at The Last Supper.

Do Catholics Worship Statues?

Any Catholic who worships a statue is misinformed because the first of the Ten Commandments clearly states, "I am the Lord your God; you shall not have strange gods before me."[64] When I was stationed in Vietnam, I would frequently see young soldiers looking at and even kissing photos of their

---

64 Excerpts from the English translation of the *Catechism of the Catholic Church* for the use in the United States of America.
Copyright © 1994. United States Catholic Conference Inc. – Liberia Editrice Vaticana. Used with permission.

wives or girlfriends. Were they worshiping those pictures? No, they were just remembering the love and honor that they had for a certain person, and they were thinking of how much they missed that individual. That is the same sort of feeling that Catholics have for statues, a rosary, medals, crosses, and holy pictures of Jesus, Mary, and the other saints. Those items help people remember something or someone in a special way.

No one thinks that people are worshipping The Tomb of the Unknown Soldier when they place wreaths on it, nor that they are worshipping King Kamehameha I when they drape leis on his statue in Honolulu. Buddhists place oranges and other foods on the graves of their ancestors. Are they worshipping those items? (Okay, every time I walk into a Krispy Kremes shop, it may seem like I'm there to worship doughnuts, but believe me, I'm not.) Many religions have their own rituals for people to honor their ancestors and deceased loved ones. It is usually not a type of worship, rather a form of remembrance and respect. It is never wrong to show respect for the dead by remembering them in some special way. To honor my family members who have died, I visit the cemetery where they're buried. Others might remember their loved ones elsewhere; some may want to just hold up a glass and toast them.

The point here is that statue worship is not what the Catholic Church teaches. Statues, pictures, and other such items are mainly a way to remember or honor someone. And I am sure that most people want to be remembered in a special way, whether at a cemetery, the mountains, or some other place.

In Hawaii, many people want to be cremated after they die and their ashes scattered in the ocean so that they might be remembered when their friends go swimming or surfing. For my part, I am already prepared to leave this world. I have my urn, carved from Hawaiian Koa wood, and a Tupperware container for the urn to be placed in, along with a note to Peg, my sister: Be sure to burp the Tupperware. Sorry, I just couldn't resist some Irish-wake humor. All kidding aside, it's important to me that I leave something behind for my loved ones to remember me by, so I've already ordered my tombstone, which reads:

Fr. Maurice George McNeely
Ordained June 7, 1958
Born February 13, 1930
Died

But I pray that I remain healthy and live long enough so that the last line on my tombstone remains blank for many years to come!

Figure 15. Photographed by the author.

"Mona by the Numbers"

Figure 16.Graphic layout by Daniel S.H. Mew.

Chapter 12

Everything Else You Wanted to Know about Catholicism but Never Had a Chance to Ask (Part 2)

In the previous chapter, I talked about how saints get their names, why we pray, and some other things that Catholics often think about. In this chapter, I'll continue that discussion with other questions that I've frequently been asked as a priest. Hopefully, this chapter will answer some of the questions that you might have.

What Is the "Eternal Now"?

Often we might wonder if we actually have free will. And if we do, then how does God know what we'll do in the future? The answer lies in the term "eternal now." We base the future on time, for example, the Earth rotating on its axis to mark days, the Earth revolving around the sun to indicate years, and so on. With God, though, there is no such thing as "time," and that is what we refer to as the eternal now.

This is not a teaching of the Church, but it's what we call a "theological conclusion." The best way for me to explain the eternal now is with the digitally created picture of "Mona by the Numbers" (see exhibit on the opposite page). The entire image is composed of myriad numbers. When you look at the picture up close, you can see each individual number, one at a time. But take a step back and look at all the numbers at once and you'll see the image of Leonardo da Vinci's famous painting, "The Mona Lisa." It's important to note that you did not make the image happen. Instead, it happened for you because you were not up close looking at each individual number.

So, what if each day in your life were like each individual number in the picture, and God was viewing it? He would be able to look closely and see your daily life as it unfolds, or He could take a step back and see the whole picture — your entire life — at once. But God wouldn't be making your life happen, just as you didn't make the image of the Mona Lisa happen when you stepped back to look at "Mona by the Numbers."

Here's another analogy. Pretend that you are standing on a hill overlooking a highway that crosses a river. You notice that a bridge over the river has been wiped out by a flood, and you see an automobile racing along the highway, approaching the washed-out bridge. Seeing this from a distance, you would know that if the car continued at that speed, it would certainly crash into the river. But, even with this knowledge, you would not be making the accident happen, although you would be able to see (and know) the outcome.

Okay, now you're probably wondering, "But can this outcome change?" And the answer is yes, and that's why prayer is so very important. God has the power to intervene through your, or other's, prayers. He must take into account, though, how a different outcome would affect the total picture. But if He chose to, He could, for instance, inspire a friend of the driver to call her on her cell phone, thus slowing her down just in time to avoid the damaged bridge.

Why Do Bad Things Happen to Good People?

If God can intervene, then why doesn't He stop bad things from happening to good people? This subject resonates a lot with me on a personal level. My oldest sister died of cancer when she was just 44 years old, leaving her husband and four young children. When she was ill, a Catholic prayer group came to the hospital and told her that, if she had faith, she would be cured. Well, I told them that they were a bunch of self-righteous bastards and that they had better not ever visit my sister again. How dare they put that guilt trip on her! She wasn't ill because of a lack of faith. In fact, she was one of the most devout and finest people I ever knew.

When people would ask her how God could allow her to be stricken with cancer, she would say, "We put additives in our food. We pollute the air. We smoke. And then we blame God for the consequences?"

In chapter 1, I told you that God cannot make us do anything. He gave humans the gift of free will, and as a result, He can't force us to be good. And that's why some people unfortunately are free to choose to do horrible things, like rape, torture, or murder others. God might intervene to prevent some of those acts — and that's why prayer is important. But if God were to intervene every time something terrible was about to occur, He would be taking away our free will, and then we wouldn't be human beings anymore.

The same applies to acts of nature. Say a tsunami were to devastate Hawaii. People might ask, "How could God allow that to happen?" Well, it was we humans who chose to build homes along the beach because we love ocean-front properties. Nature is set up for the ecological good of the entire planet. It is not set up to harm people. God might allow the tsunami to happen, but that doesn't mean He wants to hurt us or cause us to suffer. He might choose, though, not to intervene for the common good.

Have you seen the movie *Bruce Almighty*, with Jim Carey? In it, Carey's character takes over for God for a day, and in his attempt to run the universe, he tries to answer everyone's requests. He receives countless pleas to win the lottery and grants each of them. Well, as a result, every person wins but they receive just a dollar each, much to their disappointment. It's a funny scene, but the message is so important. Remember that God sees the big picture and will sometimes allow things to happen for the common good.

We should also remember that suffering and human pain are not necessarily the result of personal sin. After all, who lived a better life than Jesus and Mary? And yet they endured such tremendous pain in their lives. God allowed that to happen because He wanted us to know that He understands what we go through — that was the big picture. We humans can't see this big picture, so we don't always understand why sometimes bad things happen to good people. But we should always remember that God would never do anything to deliberately harm us. He loves us too much, more than we love ourselves. And love means doing what's best for people, even if they don't understand it at the time.

Is Cremation Allowed?

My dad always said, "Everyone wants to go to heaven, but no one wants to die." He had a point. Whenever I would ask the people in a congregation to raise their hands if they wanted to go to heaven, of course I'd see everyone's hands. But then when I would ask how many of them wanted to go there that afternoon, I'd get no takers. Yet we all know that the only way we can get into heaven is by first dying. It's ironic that we don't like to think or talk about death, even though we know that it will conquer us all one day. But you need to overcome that natural reluctance and make your wishes known on the subject.

Do you want to be cremated, or do you wish your body to be buried in a casket? This topic might be morbid and creepy, but it's important for your family to know your wishes. Some radical rebels might say, "Just throw me in the trash" or "Bury me in the backyard." Well, that might sound simple enough, but the law requires that bodies of the deceased be handled in certain ways.

In the past, the Catholic Church did not allow cremation. The belief was that it would be disrespectful to do anything to a dead body except bury it. But that view has changed and today, cremation is not only permitted, but has become a growing trend.

Still, you might wonder about the following: If my body has been turned into ashes, how will I get it back together at

148

the moment of my resurrection? That's certainly a natural concern, but we know from science that the body you have today does not contain any part that it had just seven years ago. What I mean is that the atoms in your body are continuously changing as some cells die while others are formed, so that your current body is not the same as it was seven years ago. At the moment of your resurrection, your perfect flesh and bones will be reunited with your soul, and you will live forever as a perfect human being in heaven, with God.

Another common misconception is that many people believe they will become angels in heaven. But angels are different beings, or entities, than humans. Once you come into existence as a human being, you will always remain human, and your family will always remain as your family. One of the beauties of our Catholic Christian faith is the belief that once we come into existence, we always remain in existence. What a gift for us to know this!

What Is Heaven?

To me, heaven has to be a physical place. Jesus ascended to heaven physically, Mary was taken to heaven with her physical body, and, as we say in the Creed, "I believe in the resurrection of the body and life everlasting."

It will be fun and interesting to visit with Jesus, Mary, Joseph, and all the people of history. When I get there, I want to ask Elvis Presley and Marilyn Monroe just what happened to them.

In my imagination, this is how I view heaven: Jesus, Mary, and all my relatives sitting around a big table, eating (as usual) our favorite foods, including pasties (Cornish meat-pies). And we could eat as many pizzas as we'd like and not gain an ounce. Now, that's what I call heaven! We'd all be telling our life stories, dirty jokes, and just raising hell (oops, make that, "raising heaven"), and our loud laughter and conversation would be heard all the way up to God's Holy Throne.

Here's how heaven is described in the "Catechism of the

Catholic Church" (1024): "This perfect life with the Most Holy Trinity — this communion of life and love with the Trinity, with the Virgin Mary, the angels and all the blessed — is called 'heaven.' Heaven is the ultimate end and fulfillment of the deepest human longings, the state of supreme, definitive happiness."[65]

Heaven sounds like such a remarkable place, but most of us aren't too anxious to get there this very moment. For my part, I first want to enjoy my life on earth to its fullest. Some people wonder if they will ever get to heaven, but that decision is entirely up to them. God gave us free will, and that means we may choose to be with God, or we may choose not to. So we can all eventually get to heaven if we want to. Some of us may take longer than others to arrive there, but still, you have to be the one to reject God because He will never reject you. Isn't that awesome?

Then What Is Hell?

Hell is the state of those who have rejected God. It is described by the "Catechism of the Catholic Church" (1033) in the following way: "To die in mortal sin without repenting and accepting God's merciful love means remaining separated from him forever by our own free choice. This state of definitive self-exclusion from communion with God and the blessed is called 'hell.'"[66]

Note that hell is more a state of being than a physical place. Pope John Paul II said that people should be careful in

---

[65] Excerpts from the English translation of the *Catechism of the Catholic Church* for the use in the United States of America. Copyright © 1994. United States Catholic Conference Inc. – Liberia Editrice Vaticana. Used with permission.

[66] Excerpts from the English translation of the *Catechism of the Catholic Church* for the use in the United States of America. Copyright © 1994. United States Catholic Conference Inc. – Liberia Editrice Vaticana. Used with permission.

interpreting correctly the images of hell in sacred Scripture. "Hell is the ultimate consequence of sin itself," he explained. "Rather than a place, hell indicates the state of those who freely and definitively separate themselves from God, the source of all life and joy."[67]

God in His merciful love wants everyone to choose to go to heaven, but because He gave us free will (in fact, free will is what makes us human beings), we can choose not to be there. That is, God cannot force any of us to go to heaven and be in His holy presence. At the same time, no one can be forced into hell either. According to the "Catechism of the Catholic Church" (1037), "God predestines no one to go to hell (cf. Council of Orange II [529]: DS 397; Council of Trent [1547]:1567); for this, a willful turning away from God (a mortal sin) is necessary, and persistence in it until the end."[68]

We sometimes hear the expression "eternal damnation," which is another way of saying that a person went to hell. It is the "definitive separation from God," freely chosen by an individual, and when it is confirmed with death, that seals the person's choice forever.

How many people are in hell? The Catholic Church says that it doesn't really know if even a single human being is in hell, but there has to be that possibility. Otherwise, human beings would not have the opportunity to use their God-given gift of free will to accept (or reject) God.

And What Is Purgatory?

When we were growing up, many of us were taught to pray for the poor souls in purgatory, a place of fire and physical suffering. We were told that it was where people remained until they completely made up for their sins and had been forgiven. Again, though, purgatory is more a state of being

---

[67] The Holy Father at the General Audience of Wednesday, 28 July 1999.

[68] Ibid.

than a physical place. According to Pope John Paul II, "Physical integrity is necessary to enter into perfect communion with God [in heaven]." (By "physical integrity," Pope John Paul II meant a physical body and a spiritual soul, united together.) Thus, "the term purgatory does not indicate a place but a condition of existence," where Christ "removes ... the remnant of imperfection."[69]

So, how does a person make up for his sins so that he might leave purgatory and enter heaven? Most Protestants say that all you have to do is accept Jesus as your personal savior and nothing more is needed. But suppose that after accepting Jesus, you sinned again and again. Are you not responsible for those acts? Yes, of course you are, but Catholics believe that sin can always be forgiven because of Jesus' dying on the cross for us. Nevertheless, you still need to make some amends for your personal sins. And just as we can make amends for our own sins, we can also make amends for the souls in purgatory, simply because we all belong to the mystical body of Christ. Thus, the people in heaven and on earth — as well as those in purgatory — can all help one another, and we can make amends by praying, fasting, giving alms, and doing social work.

But how do we actually know that we can help people in the state of purgatory? Catholics believe that it is a holy and pious thought to pray and to make atonements for the dead, that they might be freed from their sins. According to the Bible (2 Maccabees 12:43–45),

"He also took up a collection from all his men, totaling about four pounds of silver, and sent it to Jerusalem to provide for a sin offering. Judas did this noble thing because he believed in the resurrection of the dead. If he had not believed that the dead would be raised, it would have been foolish and useless to pray for them. In his firm and devout conviction that all of God's

---

[69] The Holy Father at the General Audience of Wednesday, August 4, 1999.

faithful people would receive a wonderful reward, Judas made provision for a sin offering to set free from their sin those who had died."[70]

Many denominations do not recognize this Scripture as being inspired, but it was always included in the Catholic Canon from the beginning. It appeared in the first Bible ever printed, the Gutenberg Bible, in 1450 A.D., which is of Catholic origin, and it also appeared in the original King James Bible in 1611 A.D., which is used by Protestants.

Is It Fair for Al Capone to Be in Heaven?

If we can all repent, even at the last moment of our lives, then can even the most depraved individuals get to heaven? That is, can Al Capone be saved? What about "The Boston Strangler" and all the other people who have committed horrific crimes? It just doesn't seem fair that such people could get to heaven, especially when you consider an old widow with 10 children who did her best to be a good wife, mother, and friend, and then she dies. Why should she receive the same reward as Al Capone, who just snuck in the back door of heaven? Or consider an unmarried teacher who devoted his entire life to helping ungrateful students, all while scraping by on a tiny wage. Why should he receive the same reward as an heiress who never helped anyone in her life and thought only of herself?

It's not wrong to be rich and to enjoy that wealth, but there is a responsibility to share with others, especially with the less fortunate. As the saying goes, "To whom much is given, much is expected in return."

And what about all those who suffered the horrors of war or died in the Holocaust? Don't they deserve something more

---

[70] Scripture taken from the Good News Translation Catholic Edition – Second Edition, Copyright © 1992, by American Bible Society. Used by permission.

in heaven than do the people who perpetuated those atrocities?

The answer is that even the most contemptible individuals can make it to heaven if they choose to be there, but they must first be purified by purgatory if they still have sins to make up for.

In heaven, though, people are treated differently. Specifically, every person there is given happiness by God according to that individual's own, fully deserving capacity. This means that there are different degrees of happiness.

Let me try to explain that with some analogies. If you give a baby a rattle, the infant could be amused for hours with the toy. The baby would be completely happy to his or her capacity. But if you give the same rattle to an adult, what happens? The grown-up would think, *boring!* Give a surfboard and a perfect wave to a surfer and that would be heaven to him. But give those same gifts to someone who can't swim and is deathly afraid of the water, and that would be hell.

We all have different ideas of happiness and different capacities for it. Likewise, in heaven, we will all be full of happiness to our own personal capacity. Only God knows what and how much that is, and He is a just God.

The concepts of the eternal now, heaven, hell, and purgatory may seem complicated and confusing, and even learned scholars struggle with them. The most important thing to remember, though, is that you can always be with God if you want to because He loves you so very much. In fact, He loves you more than you love yourself, and the only way you will go to hell (that is, the only way you will not be in His presence) is if that's your choice.

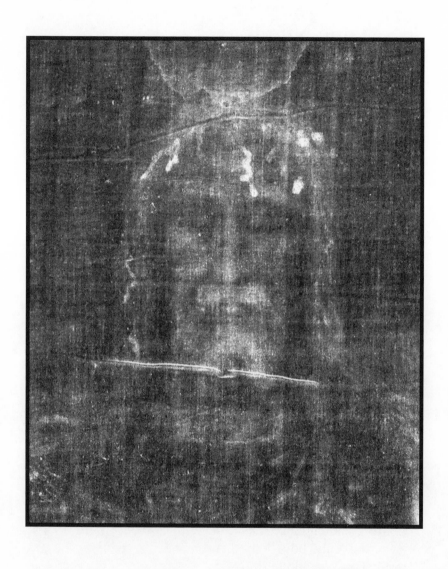

Figure 17. ©1978 Barrie M. Schwortz, All Rights Reserved.
Used with permission.

Chapter 13

Magic Numbers, "the Rapture," Psychics, and Ouija Boards

Everybody seems to have their share of superstitions. Some people try not to step on sidewalk cracks, or they'll go out of their way to avoid walking under a ladder. Others might cringe when a black cat crosses their path. In Hawaii, people are especially superstitious, perhaps because of the many gods of nature that are thought to inhabit the islands. For example, it's believed that misfortune will befall anyone who removes a lava rock from a volcano site because that act would anger Pele, a Hawaiian goddess. In this chapter, I'll discuss some of the more common superstitions — all from my personal perspective as a retired Catholic priest.

Magic Numbers

In every culture, people attribute special meanings to certain numbers that represent something other than their numerical significance. In the United States, for instance, the 12th floor of a high-rise building is usually followed by the 14th floor. Why? Because 13 is supposed to be an unlucky number. For my part, I don't think 13 is unlucky at all, perhaps because I was born on February 13, 1930. Well, that day might have been unlucky for my parents, but it sure was glorious for me as I entered this world — Ta da!

My grand entrance made the newspaper headlines because I was the only boy born that week in Wyandotte General Hospital in Wyandotte, Michigan. You would think out of all the girls born that week, at least one of them would have taken a fancy to me, but alas, none did. So maybe the number 13 might not have been the luckiest number for me after all ...

Another example was when I got back from Vietnam as a

chaplain, I saw a pretty girl walking down the street with a friend of mine. I thought I would impress them with slang that I had learned in 'Nam, so I said to the young lady, "You're a number one!"

My friend was furious! He turned to me and said, "No, asshole, she's a 10!"

I wish I could have explained to them that in Vietnam, the number one was the best and 10 was the worst — just the opposite as in the U.S. At the time, I wondered why my friend's girlfriend gave me the "stink eye" (Hawaiian slang for a nasty look). I guess it's fortunate that I became a priest, because I certainly lacked the skills for sweet-talking the opposite sex.

Throughout the Bible, references are made to symbolic numbers that held special meanings for the people of the time. There were good and bad numbers. The number 12 was thought to be good, and this is probably why Jesus chose 12 apostles, to symbolize the future goodness of their ministry. Seven was also thought to be good, and that's why there were seven days of creation. This wasn't literally true; seven was used just to represent that everything that God made was good. Six was considered a bad number because it was lacking one less than seven. So if six was bad, then multiple sixes must be really bad. That's why 666 is thought to be "the mark of the beast," or the devil's sign. But in the Bible, 666 is used to represent Caesar Nero, an unpopular ruler, and not the devil.

But in the book of Revelation, the last book of the New Testament, there are many symbolic numbers, the most famous is 666. The purpose of this book, was to give hope to the early Christians that were being persecuted by Rome. It predicted that Rome would fall and that Christianity would flourish. It was not to be taken as a future prophesy. As it states in Rev, Chapter 1 Verse 3, for the time is near when all these things will happen. When revelation was written, the people of Rome and the author would have known, that the number of the beast stands for the name of some one and the number is 666, as it states in Rev, 13, 18. The identity of the beast is Nero Caesar, an unpopular ruler, and not the devil, since the Hebrew letters for the title add up to 666. For a more complete explanation of the Book of Revelation you can refer to The Collegeville Bible Commentary, Liturgical press, Collegeville, Minnesota Pages 1265 to 1287.

I often use 666 as my lucky number just to spook superstitious people. Once, when I mentioned this in one of my sermons, an angry young man approached me after Mass and said, "That's a sin to use 666 as your lucky number! It is giving honor to the devil."

Well, I told him, "Get a life! It's just a number and God would never mess me over for any number." It's amazing how worked up some people can get over something like that.

The Rapture?

You might have heard of a novel called *Left Behind.* Written by Tim LaHaye and Jerry B. Jenkins, the book is supposed to be about earth's last days. I guess people like to read about misery because *Left Behind* is part of a series that has sold 10 million copies. But the book is based on a complete misunderstanding of Scripture. It talks about "the Rapture," a term that isn't found in Scripture. Its theory is that before the end of time (or the end of the world as we know it), Jesus will return and take a certain number of the "saved" into heaven — physically, body and soul, in an instant.

Left Behind describes a group of passengers who are traveling on a jet airplane when, all of a sudden, many are missing from their seats. One elderly lady notices that her husband, who was sitting right next to her, is gone. Only his clothes remain on the seat, terrifying her. Many others are also missing, even some children, much to the panic of the parents they've left behind. Supposedly, the missing have been taken to heaven by God. But how horrible that God would do this to the elderly woman and to those terrified parents. What anguish!

I've been thinking about why the people who were taken

159

all leave their clothing behind. Maybe the real message of the book is to always wear clean underwear because you never know when "the Rapture" will take place. Do you think I'm making fun of the book? You're darn right I am.

So many people make God out to be a bogeyman and that's such an injustice. If He loves us so much that He came down to earth and became one of us by taking on our humanity, then why would He "save" just some of us and not others? Once again, faith is a gift that not everyone receives, but if you are not given that gift then, in justice, God would not condemn you for that. According to Scripture (John 6:43–44), Jesus said, "Stop grumbling among yourselves. People cannot come to me unless the Father who sent me draws them to me; and I will raise them to life on the last day."[71]

For whatever reason, many Christians feel compelled to tell you that they are saved and that you are not. But only God and you know if you have tried to follow your own conscience to the best of your ability, and that is all that God asks for your salvation. We can be saved only by Jesus, and that applies even to those who don't know of Him. This is because of Jesus' love for everyone.

Astrology, Psychics, Fortune-Tellers, Ouija Boards and Good-Luck Charms

One day, I read my horoscope and it said, "Watch out; you may be in trouble." So I was extra cautious, just in case. Well, nothing happened. I was relieved, but hardly convinced about astrology. Once, I went with my friend to a psychic, who told me, "You don't believe." Well, the psychic was right about that — I didn't believe.

And I said, "Wow, you are a psychic!" Forgive my skepticism. The truth is that I do believe that God can give

---

[71] Scripture taken from the Good News Translation Catholic Edition – Second Edition, Copyright © 1992, by American Bible Society. Used by permission.

certain people special abilities, as He did to some of the saints. The problem is that it's difficult to figure out who really has the gift of knowing someone else's future because there are so many fakes and scam artists out there.

At the same time, we shouldn't become so cynical that we become blind to God's miracles. Remember the three wise men who came to Mary and Joseph's manger? Well, those men were astrologers, and it is said that a star brought them to the Christ child. So my personal opinion is that some individuals do have the gift of foreseeing the future, but if someone were charging me a lot of money for a palm or tarot-card reading, then I'd be highly suspicious.

I'd also be very skeptical of any objects like crystal balls or Ouija boards that are supposed to have special powers for predicting the future. That reminds me of a funny story. When I was a kid, a nun told me that using an Ouija board was a sin because it came from the devil. Being the smart-ass that I was (and maybe still am?), I told her, "You mean the devil works for Mattel?" I think I still have the bruise marks on my knuckles from the beating I took for that snide remark.

Seriously, though, I'm amazed at how many people believe their fortunes can be changed by a good-luck charm like a rabbit's foot. Well, if a rabbit's foot is so lucky, what happened to the rabbit? And, at any rate, I strongly believe that each of us has the power to exercise our own free will to change the future, so we should never resign ourselves to an unhappy fate just because a fortune-teller or Ouija board predicted that something bad would happen to us.

Relics

Catholics believe that the relics of any saint are special and that those items can help or cure people who pray with that particular saint. As such, Catholics have categorized relics into different classes. First-class relics include a saint's bones or hair. Second-class items include personal belongings (clothing, a prayer book, or rosary) or something handwritten. Some

Catholics might believe that first-class relics have more power than second-class ones, but in reality, neither have any power. It's just that first-class relics were more intimately associated with a person so they might make you feel closer to that individual.

Certainly one of the most interesting (and controversial) relics held by the Catholic Church is "The Shroud of Turin" — an ancient piece of material that some people believe was the burial cloth that enwrapped Jesus after His crucifixion. It originally came to the city of Edessa, Macedonia, where it was discovered in 544 A.D., and then moved to Constantinople (the former name of Istanbul, Turkey). Today, it resides in Turin, Italy, hence its name.

Much speculation has centered around the shroud, and it has been carbon dated several times with mixed results. Then, in January 2005, the results of additional carbon dating indicated that the "The Shroud of Turin" might actually be from the time of Jesus. If the shroud is indeed genuine, then it would be the oldest historical artifact pertaining to the life and death of Jesus.

I can understand why "The Shroud of Turin" is revered by so many people. But, as with any relic, Catholics are not required to believe in its authenticity. Still, scientists have explained that, because of chemical reactions, the shroud could contain a negative image of the person who was buried in it. As a result, if Jesus was that person, then the shroud would be the only known actual image of Him in existence.

Another revered relic or sacred site is the tomb of St. Peter, the apostle and first Pope. The tomb was discovered under the dome of St. Peter's Basilica after years of excavation. The site was far below the ground — three major levels deep — because each time the Basilica was rebuilt, the construction was done over the former shrine. On June 28, 1968, after extensive scientific investigation, Pope Paul VI announced that the relics of St. Peter had been identified with certainty. What a great gift for the Church and for all the faithful! But, once again, it is not an article of faith that you have to believe in any relic because true revelation ended with the death of the last apostle.

People who aren't Catholic sometimes think we are worshiping objects when they see us kiss or venerate a relic. But that's not the case. Instead, we are honoring the person who owned or was associated with the relic, not the object itself.

As I explained in chapter 11, people frequently honor or express their love for another person in symbolic ways. That's why a person might kiss a photo or cherish a piece of jewelry that was given by someone special. And it's why, for example, people have traveled from all over the world to the sunken U.S.S. *Arizona* in Hawaii, to pay tribute to the people who lost their lives in the Japanese attack on Pearl Harbor.

For Catholics, we can understandably be excited whenever another relic of a saint is discovered, but we should always remember that our faith is not based on such objects but on Jesus, Himself. Moreover, we should never forget the most important thing: God loves us more than we love ourselves.

Conclusion

This might be the last page of the book, but it is not the end. Rather, it's a new beginning in our quest for God and Catholic truth and knowledge. I hope it has answered a few of your questions. Most importantly, I hope it has helped address the age-old question: Why did God make me? Well, the answer to that is simple: God made you to know Him, to love Him, and to serve Him in this world, as well as to be happy with Him in the next world (heaven). First comes knowledge, next love, and finally service or dedication to Him, yourself, then toward your neighbor. Remember that it is always okay to ask questions about your faith. And never forget that your conscience is supreme and that God loves you for being you. God bless.

Special Thanks

This book is dedicated to everyone I've come in contact with throughout my entire life: all my family, relatives, and friends. You have all contributed to the making of this book, and I will be forever grateful.

I would also like to thank and pay a special tribute to my beloved parents, Catherine and Milton McNeely, and to all my ancestors who came before me, as well as the relatives whom I met as a youngster. Their influence has helped to mold me into the rascal person I am today. I am also indebted to Monsignor Roy Peters for his inspiration as a living example of what a true and dedicated priest should be. I have met so many dear people and have been blessed to have them in my life, including

All my classmates and the faculty from St. Vincent DePaul High School in Detroit,

St. Jerome's College in Kitchner, Ontario,

St. Paul Seminary in St. Paul, Minnesota,

My Michigan family and friends,

My North Dakota family and friends,

The clergy of the diocese of Bismarck,

Parishioners and friends of St. Joseph Parish of Mandan, Christ the King of Mandan, St. Leo Parish of Minot, Bishop Ryan High School of Minot, St. Vincent's of Mott, St. Bridget's of Parshall, Sacred Heart of Plaza, The Immaculate Heart of Mary of Marmarth, and St. Mels of Rhame,

My military family and friends,

Fellow chaplains, parishioners, and friends of Ft. Rucker, Alabama,

All my fellow military members in Vietnam,

Parishioners and friends of Ft. DeRussy, Ft. Shafter, and

Tripler Army Medical Center, Honolulu, Hawaii; Ft. Benning, Georgia; and Ft. Carson, Colorado,

My family and friends in Hawaii, including the bishop and priests of the diocese of Honolulu, parishioners and friends of Our Lady of Peace Cathedral in Honolulu, Our Lady of the Mount in Honolulu, Holy Family Church in Honolulu, and Holy Family Catholic Academy in Honolulu, and

My Las Vegas family and friends, including the clergy of the diocese of Las Vegas, and the rector, staff, and volunteers of the Shrine of the Most Holy Redeemer, Las Vegas.

I wish I could mention people by their proper names in this book because each one of you is so important in my life, but there just wouldn't be enough space. I know that you know who you are, and I will continue to remember you in my daily Mass. I am forever grateful.

Sincerely yours in Christ,
Father Mac

About the Author

Fr. McNeely was ordained a Catholic priest in his hometown of Detroit. He has served as a priest in many capacities — parish priest, pastor, prison ministry, hospital chaplain, and army chaplain. His down-to-earth sermons incorporating his sense of humor have made him popular with Catholics and non-Catholics of all ages. He has the keen ability to make the Catholic Church's teachings easier to understand. Father McNeely is currently retired and resides in Las Vegas. He continues to be active as a priest at The Shrine of the Most Holy Redeemer.

Copyright and Acknowledgments

Bibliography

Elders' Journal of the Church of Jesus Christ of Latter-day Saints, Vol. 1, No. 3, July 1838. Far West, Caldwell, Missouri by the Church of Jesus Christ of Latter-day Saints. SolomanSpaldingDotCom. Special Collections: Early Mormonism Collection 2, http://www.solomonspalding.com/docs/eldjur03.htm (accessed August 26, 2005).

Rich, Tracey R. "What do Jews Believe?" in "Judaism 101," http://www.jewfaq.org/beliefs.htm (accessed August 19, 2005).

"Aimee Semple McPherson" in Wikipedia, http://en.wikipedia.org/wiki/Aimee_Semple_McPherson (accessed August 19, 2005).

http://www.lds.org/ (accessed August 19, 2005).

Midbon, Mark, "A Day without Yesterday: Georges Lemaitre & the Big Bang" in Catholic Educator's Resource Center, http://catholiceducation.org/articles/science/sc0022.html (accessed August 19, 2005).

"The Church of Scientology" in The Religious Movements Homepage at the University of Virginia, http://religiousmovements.lib.virginia.edu/nrms/scientology.html (accessed August 19, 2005).

"Jehovah's Witnesses" in The Religious Movements Homepage at the University of Virginia, http://religiousmovements.lib.virginia.edu/nrms/Jwitness.html (accessed August 19, 2005).

"Islam" in The Religious Movements Homepage at the University of Virginia, http://religiousmovements.lib.virginia.edu/nrms/islam.html (accessed August 19, 2005).

Linder, Doug. "The Vatican's View of Evolution; The Story of Two Popes" in University of Missouri-Kansas City School of Law. 2004. http://www.law.umkc.edu/faculty/projects/ftrials/conlaw/vaticanview.html (accessed August 19, 2005).

Mcleod, Melvin. Shambhala Sun article, "You Can't Attend Your Own Funeral," Buddhism Culture Meditation Life. 2000.

The Catholic University of America. *New Catholic Encyclopedia*, Volume IV, New York, New York:McGraw-Hill. 1967.

The Catholic University of America. *New Catholic Encyclopedia*, Volume X, New York, New York:McGraw-Hill. 1967.

Berg, Michael. *Becoming Like God Kabbalah and Our Ultimate Destiny*. New York, New York:Kabbalah Centre International. 2004.

Benzinger Brothers Inc. *Summa Theologica of Thomas Aquinas*, Vol. 2. 1947.

O'Gorman, B. and M. Faulkner. *The Complete Idiot's Guide to Understanding Catholicism*, Second Edition: Alpha Press. 2003.

Walker, C. and J. Shankar. "Which Ten Commandments?" (accessed August 19, 2005).

"New World Translation of the Holy Scriptures." Brooklyn, New York:Watchtower Bible and Tract Society of Pennsylvania. 1981.

McConkie, Bruce. *Mormon Doctrine*, Second Edition. Salt Lake City, Utah:Deseret Book Co. 1966.

"What Is Scientology? The Comprehensive Reference on the World's Fastest Growing Religion," Los Angeles:Bridge Publications Inc. 1992.

Smith, J.F. *Teaching of the Prophet Joseph Smith*. Salt Lake City, Utah:Deseret Book Company. 1976.